THE LOGOS OF HERACLITUS

THE LOGOS OF

HERACLITUS

THE FIRST PHILOSOPHER OF THE WEST ON ITS MOST INTERESTING TERM

EVA BRANN

PAUL DRY BOOKS   PHILADELPHIA 2011

First Paul Dry Books Edition, 2011

Paul Dry Books, Inc.
Philadelphia, Pennsylvania
www.pauldrybooks.com

Text type: Sabon
Display type: Lithos and Stone Sans
Designed and composed by P. M. Gordon Associates
Cover design by Marcy Coffey, Willie • Fetchko Graphic Design

Printed in the United States of America

Library of Congress Cataloging-in-Publication Data

Brann, Eva T. H.
  The logos of Heraclitus : the first philosopher of the West on its
most interesting term / Eva Brann. — 1st Paul Dry Books ed.
      p. cm.
  Includes bibliographical references (p.   ) and index.
  ISBN 978-1-58988-070-2 (alk. paper)
  1. Heraclitus, of Ephesus. 2. Logos (Philosophy). I. Title.
  B224.L6B73 2011
  182'.4—dc23
                                               2011024253

Also by Eva Brann

TO SUSAN FOOTE AND STEVE FEINBERG

For mornings of unforgettable beauty
and evenings of memorable conversation

My warm thanks to
Kaura Mackey and Timothy Reilly,
who, being excellent students of my college,
were remarkably adept at dealing with this manuscript.

CONTENTS

LIST OF FIGURES

THE LOGOS OF HERACLITUS

Figure 1. "Heraclitus" from Raphael, School of Athens.

I

THE FIGURE OF HERACLITUS

Front and just off-center, in the lower foreground of Raphael's fresco *The School of Athens*, sits a massive, looming, hirsute figure, brooding and withdrawn from all his philosophical schoolmates (Figure 1). He stares downwards and inwards, and for the moment, he is also turned away from the stack of papers over which his pen is poised: Heraclitus. All the others, the whole assembly of Pre- and Post-Socratics, are in communication with each other, speaking, listening, or signifying by gesture, as do the two central figures above, Plato and Aristotle—the one pointing upwards, the other down (Figure 2).

Over on the opposite wall of the Stanza della Segnatura in the Vatican, Raphael has depicted a "disputation" of Saints and Doctors, centered about the mystery of the Eucharist (Figure 3). The figures closest to the

Figure 2. Raphael, School of Athens.

Figure 3. Raphael, Disputation on the Holy Sacrament.

center, the altar that carries the Host, point to it, but their heads are turned and their speech is addressed to their followers behind them, who are talking among themselves.[1]

Raphael seems to have had a most acute sense for the addresses of human speech: to or at, like- or averse-minded, signifying or articulating, connecting in agreement or contention, with contemporaries or across time, by speaking silence or reticent writing. His philosophers talk *to* each other, together in one timeless place. His doctors talk *at* their disciples, divided by the two-sided space. Heraclitus has turned out of the picture, but he looks *within*. There he finds the Logos, the order that is the cosmos—the world without—whose mouthpiece and scribe he means to be.

That *is* Heraclitus, an engaged solitary, an inward-turned observer of the world, inventor of the first of philosophical genres, the thought-compacted aphorism, prose that could contend with poetry. It is linguistically ingenious, teasingly obscure in reputation, but hard-hittingly clear in fact. Each saying contains a concentrated drop of meaning—the kind of writing one *would* often stop to look away from. Such a style, tense and beautiful, seems to be favored by people who find harsh realism exhilarating. The ancient Spartans, Hobbes, and Nietzsche are examples; its mood is now tersely mordant, now generously humane.

Nothing, however, is firm about his writing, his "composition," his *syngramma*, as Aristotle refers to it (*Rhetoric* 1407b): Was it a continuous treatise whose aphoristic impression—he did not, of course, write "fragments," though concision and incompleteness suits his style—is a byproduct of the fragmentary transmission or a random stack of occasional notes or, as I think, a well-conceived collection of sayings? We don't even know the title. The collection is supposed to have been called "On Nature," which might be translated as "On the Moving World," but that is the title imputed to many an early work.[2]

Nor is the time of his writing relative to his great antagonist—his fraternal antagonist, I should say—known for certain: Did Heraclitus from eastern Ephesus incite Parmenides from western Elea to propose his seamless sphere of Being in opposition to the former's river of Becoming (as I think), or was Parmenides the first philosopher and Heraclitus the first opponent? What, indeed, could it mean to be the first philosopher (see Section III U, "The Being of Parmenides")?[3] An aside: My priority implies that our philosophical West began in Asia Minor. Well, so did our poetical West—Homer. Perhaps being betwixt and between has generative power.

Furthermore, the true relation between the two originating protagonists of our Western tradition cannot be conclusively established: Are they, as I have intimated, about the same business or are they poles apart?

Nor is there certainty in the ascertaining, ordering, and interpreting of the fragments—least of all about the last, of course. What part of the source-context, of each of the many texts from which the fragments are culled, is exact quotation, what part referring citation, what part adaptive paraphrase? In what order do these wholes or snippets stand in the original composition? But always and above all, what did Heraclitus mean?

About the meaning only this much is not disputed: that *logos* is Heraclitus's key word. I think he retains in it an old, and also gives to it a distinctively new, meaning, though what that latter might be is very much under debate. Translations run from "word" to "world-principle," from "sense" to "universal law."[4]

The upshot is that no interpretation has prevailed; every question is wide open. And no wonder: Even in antiquity Heraclitus was called "the Obscure, the Dark" (*ho skoteinos*). Socrates is reported to have said, after Euripides had given him Heraclitus's composition—there is a nice frisson in imagining Socrates reading a Pre-Socratic[5]—that what he understood was genuinely fine and that he thought the rest must be just as fine "but it wants a Delian diver." Perhaps he meant that these divers go into the dark deep to bring up pearls. Or was he referring to the Pythagoreans who were spoken of as Delian divers?—if he was connecting *them* to Heraclitus, it will turn out to be significant (Section III H).

At any rate, whoever is captivated by the revelatory riddlings and brilliant obscurities of what remains of Heraclitus has to begin anew—accepting help, to be sure, from previous readings—in a spirit of receptivity *and* reserve. But essentially everyone must pester the supposed obscurantist until he opens up. Heraclitus is no less and no more pregnantly dark than an oracle, and perhaps he did in fact appropriate Apollo's style:

The Lord whose oracle is in Delphi neither speaks
nor hides but signifies. (93)[6]

Apollo, however, was the light-god and his oracles were
meant to yield their significance eventually, to be inter-
pretable. Besides, Heraclitus is not always obscure; he
is sometimes as wittily bald as solitaries in particular
can be.

Would he laugh at our efforts at sense-making, I
wonder, with the unamused laughter of one also known
as "the Weeping Philosopher"? He certainly blew hot
and cold on his fellow-Ephesians, now as one casting his
pearls before swine, and then again as one repeatedly
asserting the common character of a *logos* available to
all human beings (Section V).

II

THE WORD
LOGOS

Logos is, I think, not only Heraclitus's key word, but that of the Western philosophical tradition, which acts *as* a tradition because its moments are both bound together and driven apart by dialogue: the back-and-forth of the *logos*. This dialogue had its first great episode, mentioned above, between Heraclitus and Parmenides, no matter who spoke first or whether they literally spoke to each other. I am discounting here Heraclitus's neighbors to the south on the coast of Asia Minor. Those men from Miletus were called the "Physicists" by Aristotle because they searched for, and fixed on, the material that might most eminently function to support the various motions and transformations seen in the world (Section III I).[1] They each settled on a "stuff" that appeared before the senses in some familiar form or before the mind as a fairly immediate abstraction. Heraclitus

9

seems to have despised them. We can only speculate on the reasons, which I imagine to have lain in the incoherence of their principles. In any case, there wasn't a dialogue; they weren't contenders in the realm of *logos*. Yet they might have incited in Heraclitus an ambition to go deeper, and so they were perhaps in a sort of proto-dialectic with him after all.

What *logos* means to Heraclitus will be the main business of this book, but for thinking about that I should go briefly into what *logos* meant to those using the word before and after him. A first survey of the activities that *logos* spans yields: collecting and laying-down, tale-telling and relating, counting and account-giving, arguing, and, so, speaking, saying, and above all, the thinking, the reasoning, that is behind uttering—and finally also writing.

However, the first, etymologically most original meaning, not entirely lost in common usage, goes back to the verb *legein* on which the noun *logos* is based. It first meant: to pick up and lay down or lay by, that is, to col*lect*, hence to count up, to tell (as does a bank teller), to re-count (as in a tale), and thus to give an account.[2]

Thence come a multitude of meanings connected to speech, especially as it is the vehicle for human rationality, both as the thought itself and the utterance that tells it, the word that focuses it, the saying that expresses it, the sentence that states it, the sense or meaning it conveys, as well as the explanation that expands and the argument that enforces it. In fact, Latin *ratio*, whence comes our "reason," translates *logos*. Furthermore, in English as well, telling is relating, that is, referring to events through speech, naming them, and keeping in memory the people associated with them; thus *logos* means "fame," and is used that way by Heraclitus once (112). But the sense most significant here is that of "addressing," of entering into relations: The *logos* brings terms into relations to each other, particularly the ratio-relation that connects two terms in mutually determining juxtaposition, especially in respect to their common measurability; *logos* names a relation of magnitudes. I am assuming here that this meaning was being brought into use by Pythagoras, the founder of Western mathematics, just before Heraclitus wrote. Heraclitus, ever the greatly absorptive despiser, mentions him—denigratingly—twice, as he does Homer, whom he offers to "thrash" (42). And yet Homer too is, surreptitiously, a model—a model, because it is not thinkable that Heraclitus's novel use of analogy did not owe something to Homeric metaphor (Section III O). Metaphor is, after all, the pervasive Homeric element, and metaphor says poetically what analogy says prosaically; the thought-structure is the same. Thus, incidentally, Heraclitus does quite deliberately what we are so frequently directed to do these days: think nonlinearly, "outside the box." Analogical thinking is not news.

Homer also preserves the aboriginal "collecting" meaning of the *logos* verb, together with the "telling":

Let us gather (*legomen*) the bones of Patroclos,

says Achilles, the bones of that kind man who, just before calamity struck, had

> delighted him [a wounded warrior] with tales
> (*logoi*). (*Iliad* 23.239, 25.393)

After Heraclitus, *logos* gathered more and more uses; Liddell and Scott's *Greek-English Lexicon* gives five dense columns under ten general headings. The emphasis on the "logical" use increases and so also its aforesaid employment for linguistic structures from the single word (name) to a sentence (proposition), and a paragraph (argument). Both verb and noun acquire prepositional prefixes, of which the most weighty in this context (Section III E) is ana-*logia* (proportion), already mentioned; the most frequent in English, the "-logy" and "-logist" endings that designate a study or science and those who pursue it. (Aristotle uses the term *physiologoi* exchangeably with *physikoi* of those concerned with accounting for natural motion. For us physiology and physics, the sciences respectively of bodies moving with life or by force, have diverged.) Finally, there is that most future-fraught verb *dia-legesthai* ("to talk things through, to converse, to speak with—or against—one another"); the verb is in the "middle voice," which betokens turn-and-turn-about, that is, reflexivity, coming together, even in opposition, in a dialogue; hence "dialectic," which will come to name the powerful engine of developing rational thought as it posits, opposes, and composes itself.

To return to *logos*: It comes to mean *The Word* that is from and with God, thus, *The Son*. Heraclitus will play a role in this future use (Section IV), since he will give *logos* a novel, elevated sense that works its way down the centuries; his is a remote precursor of the Christian use.

From now on I will write Logos or The Logos without italics for the Heraclitean term, otherwise italic *logos* to betoken the Greek word in its various other uses, or even plain logos to signify that the word might as well be regarded as having passed into English.

III

THE LOGOS OF HERACLITUS

A. Logos and *logos*

Thus for *logos*, at least, I will be eschewing translation in favor of transcription; circumscription of Heraclitus's meaning is the best I can do. Here is the fragment most clearly relevant to that effort, first in transcribed Greek, then in a standard translation:

> *ouk emou, alla tou logou akousantas homologein*
> sophon estin hen panta [*éinai*]
>
> Listening not to me but to the Logos, it is wise to acknowledge that all things are one. (50)

This is as tricky a Heraclitean saying as has survived. How remarkable it is comes out when we compare it to something apparently similar that Socrates says in

Plato's *Republic*: "What difference is it to you whether it seems so to *me* or not, when *you* haven't tested out the argument (*ton logon*)?" (349a). Or in the *Phaedo* "If . . . you give little thought to Socrates and much more to the truth, you must agree with me (*syn-homo-logesate*) if I seem to say what's true" (91c). These speeches are straightforward exhortations to doing one's own thinking, in search of—an as yet unspecified—truth. Heraclitus means worlds more. He directs us not to intellectual self-reliance, not to seek *some* truth, but to comprehend and follow *this* truth: that said by the Logos. To convey this truth, Heraclitus expresses himself with canny ambivalence. So I will try my hand at conveying it:

> For those hearing not *me* but *the Saying*, to say the same is the Wise Thing: Everything [is] One.
> (my italics)

"The Saying," a precious usage—it could be "the Speech," but that's no better—must be forgiven, because it works so well here. It translates "The Logos" and brings out not only that in one aspect it appears as humanly receivable utterance of wisdom but also that we—I think he means us—are obligated literally to "*homo-logein*," "to say the same" (the ordinary meaning is "to agree"). "Hear" translates a plural participle *akousantas* from the verb for hearing, listening, heeding (whence our "acoustics"). Thus the verb also means "to obey," as when a parent says "Don't you hear me? Why don't you listen?" (The German adjective *hörig* means being a slave to someone.) "Hearing" is in the aorist aspect, a kind of past that betokens a once-and-for-all situation, as that of people who have really taken in a maxim. To hear it is to get it.

Next, "the Wise Thing" (*to sophon*), in Greek as in the English translation, hints of facing in two directions: It is, to be sure, wise for the people who do obey the Logos to agree to its saying, but what it says (perhaps even *is*)—that saying itself, which they are to repeat—*is* the Wise Thing. It is both a maxim and Wisdom Incarnate.

Here is the Saying's announcement:

One : Everything (or "one : all," *hen : panta*).

Hen, the neuter singular of "one," betokens unity; *to hen*, the substantive, is the mathematical word for unity. *Panta* the neuter plural of *pan*, "all," can mean "all things" or, distributively, "everything." Below I shall translate it either way, depending on whether Heraclitus seems to me to be speaking a shade more collectively or more severally. The "is" is a scholarly emendation and ruins the juxtaposition, so I've bracketed it.[1] And finally, this Logos is not only a Speech but a Speaker, for he is audible to us.

So now:

Listening not to me but to The Speaker, there is a Wise Thing to agree with—One : Everything.

Nevertheless, in Greek the fragment begins with Heraclitus: "Not to *me* . . ." This is a *proud* subordination of a man to Logos. Consequently he sometimes seems to be propounding riddles, for he is attempting to render the Logos's Saying to himself verbatim, as it were—himself both faithful listener and chosen speaker.

I have no doubt that Heraclitus intended all the possibilities, and intended them all at once, not from sheer linguistic agility, but because his style of aphoristic succinctness, exploded by punning resonances, so exactly conveys his discovery: the all-at-onceness of all things in their multiplicity—lightly girdled speech sweeping along vast skirts of significance.

Here is my meaning-expansion of the fragment: "I myself am saying this; it is my *logos*. But in hearing me speak, listen not to the Heraclitus who is talking but to *the* Speaker whose Saying I am uttering, having heard and heeded him—as should you. Then you too will say, along with me and 'him'—for I am telling of a power that addresses us—that there is Something Wise, which it is wise for us to say along with the Logos and in agreement with it, because it is found embodied in our world: There is a Unity relating Everything and All Things."

I will shortly try to show what this Wise Thing is—it *is* actually the Logos himself—and what it does, and how it works by means of *logoi* (plural of *logos*) to bring everything to unity, to oneness. This is what Heraclitus has heard and heeded—we would say, discovered. Or, more daringly: If to be addressed by a voice both from within and from beyond the world is to receive a revelation, then Heraclitus was such a recipient. That would account for an observation Aristotle makes of Heraclitus somewhat out of the blue—that he was as convinced of what he *believed* as others are of what they *know* (*Nicomachean Ethics* 1146b).

B. The Wise Thing

I can't think of an elegant way to translate this neuter singular adjective that Heraclitus writes either with or without an article; *to sophon*, or just *sophon*. It is not someone's wisdom, though it teeters on the edge:

> One thing is the Wise—to understand the maxim (*gnome*) by which everything is steered (*kybernatai*) through everything. (41, but taking the verb as passive; see W 120)

That sounds as if human understanding were meant: There is a maxim, a practical principle, in short a "gnome" (actually an English word meaning an aphoristically, pithily expressed *know*ledge, judgment, opinion, or insight) that it is uniquely wise for us to know since it governs the relation of all things to everything. But:

> Human kind does not have [such] insights (*gnomas*); the divine has [them]. (78)

So neither can this one maxim (the one mentioned in Fragment 41) be *our* wisdom. For it is the design—

gnome can also mean "design" in the sense of "intention"—that, being one, administers unity—that steers, controls, governs the way *in which*, and indeed *the fact that*, everything is related to everything. (From the verb *kybernan*, akin to our "govern," come all the cyberwords of our control-speak.) But careful! The verb "is steered" is not necessarily passive; it can be read as the middle voice; and then it means "steers itself," the world is self-steered; its Wisdom is inherent.

Moreover:

Of all whose *logoi* I have heard, not one has
come this far—to know that "Wise" is separated
(*kechorismenon*) from everything. (108)

And finally:

The Wise Thing, one and only, wants and does not
want to be called by the name of Zeus. (32)

So this Wise Thing is both separated *from* all things and is also at work *within* everything as well as *on* itself. It is both disposer and structure. It is, as philosophers now say, both transcendent and immanent. When you speak of it, when you address it, you may call it by the name of a divinity, the chief one of the Olympians, but that would be something of a transgression. It isn't *a* god and doesn't want to be personalized. And yet—its being is a *gnome*, a judgment, which also means "purpose, intention." The cosmic Wise Thing has *intention*.

But how does Heraclitus, a man among men, know all this? He, at least, has listened to the Logos, Speaker and Speech, Uttered Wisdom.

And he has passed its saying on to us. Have we been spoken to ambivalently, "double-valuedly"? Yes, but not ambiguously, indistinctly. What comes through clearly is this: Our *logos* and our *logoi*, the sense we receive and the words we in turn say, should be informed by our having heard *the* Logos. This great Logos has a wisdom, or rather it *is* the Wise Thing, and this Wise Thing has a maxim, or rather it *is* that practical principle which guides everything through everything, relates all things to all things, which says One : Everything. Why does the Logos express himself, itself, in this double way? With that way of asking—asking, that is, as if ambivalence might be not the puzzle but the key—I am, I think, on the path to an interpretation of Heraclitus's Logos.

C. The Common

But first a look at a feature of the Logos vis-à-vis the listener, one that concerns Heraclitus's own preoccupation: *Who* can know and does know *what*? The fragment that most bears on this question is the one that Aristotle speaks of as standing at the beginning of the "composition" (*Rhetoric* 407b):

Men become (or, are born) unapprehending (or unmindful, *axynetoi*) of the Logos that ever is, both

before they have heard it and having first heard it.
(1, first sentence)

As so often, *both* senses are to be heard: that humans
are *at birth* deaf to the Logos that is always present
and that they *become unmindful* in the course of ordinary living; even those who have been told but haven't
listened.

Of these latter, Heraclitus says that they are

unapprehending (*axynetoi*) even when they've
heard, similar to the deaf. The proverb is witness to
their being "absent though present." (34)

And probably close to Fragment 1 came:

Therefore one must follow what is the Common (*toi
xynoi*). But although the Logos is common (*xynou*)
the many live as if they had a private mind (*phronesin*, in the sense of mindful insight). (2)

There is a riotous triple punning here: *xynos* (Ionian
Greek for Attic *koinos* "common") is intended to reso-
nate with *xyn noi*, "with intellect" and also with *axynetoi*, "unapprehending" in Fragment 1.

Is this serious business, punning being held in low
esteem by earnest folk? "He that would pun would
pick a pocket" (Pope). Puns are homonyms, words the
same in sound but diverse in meaning. Here is an example from one of Heraclitus's successors in verbal agility,
Will Shakespeare:

Whoever hath her wish, thou hast thy Will
And Will to boot, and Will in overplus.
(Sonnet 135)

Because they are made-to-order verbal representations of the "one:everything," or at least the "one-many" principle, "homonyming" is a way to *homologein*, to say: "One relates many." Once again I have the sense that the punning mode was very much Heraclitus's own—and yet appropriated, perhaps from the great oracle at Delphi which excelled not in shimmering ambiguity but in fixed equivocation: clear meanings, but two at once.[2] Heraclitus points it out:

The Lord, whose is the Oracle at Delphi, neither speaks nor hides but signifies (*semainei*). (93)

A pun also gives a sign; its sound or look shows more than what it seems primarily to say. I want to claim that Heraclitus's puns and his paradoxes are his double way of being double-tongued, that they are complementary. His puns insinuate diverse meanings into one word-sound; his paradoxes force opposing facts into one verbal assertion (Section III R).

In this case, in Fragment 2, Heraclitus relates intelligence and its opposite, lack of apprehension, to "the Common," by one (approximate) sound. Again, even this "common" is to be heard in two aspects. On the one hand, there is *the* Common, our world and the wise plan that holds it together, the Logos that always is, that both works in the world and speaks to all from beyond it. On the other hand, there are some who hear and heed it, and to whom it *is* common, but more who are deaf and inattentive—unapprehending. They have a private mind, *idian phronesin* (*idios*, "private," is the adjective from which we get our word "idiot"); they are "though present, absent;" as we say, they are "not all there," out of it—"common-less." To Heraclitus it is a scandal that the world's governor speaks to us *out of* the cosmos and *about* it, that its wise plan is patent within it, that the message is utterly common both in the sense of being everywhere, being always the same, and being for us— and yet people go off on their own—idiot minds:

> That Logos with which they keep company most continuously, the one who manages the whole— with that they are at variance, and things they meet with every day—those appear strange to them. (72)

These folks, moreover, who are absent from the world they live in are, it turns out, doubly private, de- prived. For what

> they do awake slips by them, just as when asleep it slips their memory (end of 1)

—the lapsing of memory piled on lack of awareness. Heraclitus finds human incomprehension in a world comprehended by the Logos pretty incomprehensible.

So this philosophical loner—that, at least, was the tradition about him[3]—sits aloof, as in the *School of Athens*, alone in the cause of the common logos that speaks to all about what belongs to all but is heard and heeded so far by him alone. I think this sense, that truth lies most patent in what is most ordinary and is for that very reason least apprehended, is the first motive of philosophy. Socrates, that Post-Heraclitean, will call it "wonder": "For that is the special affect of the lover of wisdom (*philosophos*)—wondering" (*Theatetus* 155d). There is, to be sure, a difference. Heraclitus observes the Common surrounding us all and *blames* humankind for being estranged from it; Socrates tries to *induce* a sense of estrangement from what we take for granted around us—that is what his wonder is. This difference betokens the directions in which philosophy is to lead: *into* the cosmos for Heraclitus, *out of* the world for Socrates— Raphael's Plato points upwards.

Heraclitus, however, scorns those many who are least aware of what is most theirs, not because they are incapable, but just because they *are* capable:

Thinking is common to all. (113)

He does not betray cosmic commonality even in his scorn for what is humanly all-too-common. He insists on the universality of sane humanity even in the face of ordinary retreat into the privations of willful privacy:

It belongs to all men to know themselves and to be soundminded. (116)

Here is the antecedent of the injunction "Know Thyself" that Socrates borrowed from the Temple at Delphi: With Heraclitus it is original, for we know that there was no standing temple at Delphi in his lifetime; Herodotus says so (*Persian Wars* 1.50, 5.52). This is the divine wisdom in which, for both philosophers, intellectual insight is conjoined with moral excellence. Heraclitus takes very seriously this inward-turning to meet the cosmos (Section V). As he will again and again be shown to be double-tongued, so he is consistently two-faced—the original Janus-faced philosopher.

Meanwhile there is no getting around his high predicament, the fact already noticed, that a logos-teller speaks both as *this* human being, that is, originally— and Heraclitus is an original if ever there was one—and yet not for himself, for he has to "say the same" as the Logos. That is what it means to speak truths, a word that occurs only once in the fragments:

> To be soundminded: the greatest excellence; and wisdom: to say and do true things, giving heed according to nature. (112)

This fragment brings out the above-mentioned relation of truth, virtue, and deeds (Section V), but it also specifies where and how truth is to be found—in nature *and* in the Logos, which it is in accord with—because it is of the Logos's devising; hence Heraclitus must expound words and deeds as the common-less cannot:

dividing each thing according to nature and declaring its relation [to others]. (Part of 1)

There is no room here for the self-regarding vice of *personal* philosophical originality.

The Logos, however, speaks with a double tongue and thus doubly to and through Heraclitus. Thence issue logical contradictions (of which more later, Section III R). But first, the Logos is, as I intimated, not only double-tongued but also two-faced: It shows one aspect within, another without the cosmos. Consequently Heraclitus too is cognitively comprehensive:

A wisdom-loving man must be inquiring into many things. (35)

"Wisdom-loving" translates *philosophos*. (If I dared, I'd translate it "wannabe-wise" as opposed to *sophos*, "having smarts," skillful.) "Inquiring" is *historas*, participle of the verb from which comes *historia*, which by Herodotus's agency came to mean the study of the past—though not yet for Heraclitus.

But he also says:

Much-learnedness (*polymathia*) does not teach one to have intellectual insight (*noos*). (40)

On the one hand, you have to be keenly and extensively observant to see the Logos at work in—or as—nature; on the other, heaps of learning lead to knowing everything and nothing. It drowns out the Logos.

I think that Heraclitus was the first Westerner to ponder how thought and world come to jibe: A Logos that we can hear must be the designer *and* the design of the world.

D. The Discovery of Pythagoras

Fragment 40 continues:

> For it would have taught Hesiod and Pythagoras
> and further Xenophanes and Hecataeus. (end of 40)

Here is deployed the Heraclitean mode noticed above: unacknowledged appropriation; you might call it creative ingratitude. *Logos* can both bestow and mean fame; by the same token it can defame. Surely Heraclitus did in fact learn something from Hesiod; Xenophanes was said to have actually been his teacher; and he was, possibly, personally associated with a putative Pythagorean. Yet he defamed them lustily. He is supposed to have said that "he listened to no one"; which has the overt meaning in Greek of attending to no one's lectures and here the implied sense of "heeding only the Logos."[4] This intent listening to the Logos made him a recalcitrant learner from his fellows. He appropriated with averted consciousness.

Pythagoras was born in 570 B.C.E., a "long" generation, about 35 years, before Heraclitus. He *could* have been his teacher, not in the sense that Heraclitus was a listener in on Pythagoras's so-called "oral teachings," but rather by way of influence, as we say. It *is* a strange fact that the early testimony about Pythagoras comes largely from a few Heraclitean fragments. That he *was* Heraclitus's teacher, both scorned and studied, having a part in the shaping of the central Heraclitean terms, both the Logos and subsidiary *logoi*, I am about to claim. Indeed, the abuse Heraclitus heaps on him might attest to some sort of intimacy; it feels that way. Here is how the ancient source introduces the relevant fragment: "The physicist Heraclitus all but croaks and says:"

> Pythagoras, son of Mnesarchus, did practice inquiry especially among all men, and, having picked out for himself these compositions, he made a wisdom of his own, a multi-learning, an ill-skill (*polymathie, kakotechnie*). (By 17)[5]

You can tell the spiteful delight the aphorist took in his two word-inventions.

If Heraclitus was the first philosophical philosopher, it may be that there was an earlier, a mathematical philosopher—Pythagoras, who is indeed credited with the introduction of the word "philosophy"—and that he opened the way. Nonetheless, in defense of my subtitle, which credits Heraclitus with being the *first* philosopher (see also Section III U), Heraclitus was, perhaps maliciously, not far off the mark in implicitly taking Pythagoras's *philosophia*, "the love of *sophia*," as an attachment to mere *techne*, "skill, craft." As I said, the early meaning of *sophia* was just that: "skill, crafty know-how." Yet I think that he showed Heraclitus how his Logos might assert its unifying function.

Then what exactly did Heraclitus have against Pythagoras? I conjecture that he means by *kakotechnie* "bad-skill" or "low-skill," not as opposed to high-tech, but as we sometimes feel compelled to speak of "boorscientists," unreflective number-crunchers. Perhaps Pythagoras put his newly discovered *logoi* and their *analogia* to too narrow a use for Heraclitus, who had more cosmic applications in mind. And indeed, the latter uses the word *kosmos* often, in the sense of physical worldorder: It is a sense whose appropriation for cosmology from its ordinary meanings of order and ornament is, as it happens, also attributed to Pythagoras. *Philosophos* and *kosmos* are respectively the designations of Heraclitus's own life and world—no insignificant spoils pillaged from Pythagoras, these two future-laden terms of our West.

What was it that Heraclitus needed that Pythagoras had worked out? One might say that it was a quantified version of metaphor, the verbal figure that is the mainstay of Homer's poetry. In the *Poetics*, Aristotle analyzed its structure as analogical and evidently gave it its Greek name, metaphor, which means "carry-over" (1457b).

In metaphors generally, *as* a this is said to be related to a that, *so* this other is related to that other. In Homeric metaphors specifically, that other tends to precede: As an image of absent off-site things has certain internal relations, so do things present to view. This "carry-over" is permitted by a sameness in difference;

it is the poet's talent to discern such sameness. Here is one of Homer's loveliest metaphors in an impoverished paraphrase that brings out its metaphor-structure:

As in heaven the stars shine so splendidly,
So in the plain of Troy shone the Trojan campfires.
(*Iliad* 8.555)

Heraclitus, the equal-opportunity despiser of poets and mathematicians, nonetheless needs and uses metaphors; they perfectly suit the expression of his way of thinking and the construction of his cosmos—by the bond of all-pervasive *logoi*.[6]

E. *logoi* and *analogia*

The discovery of Pythagoras and those around him was, one might say, a metaphorical structure in musical sound: If two strings of equal weights but of different measured lengths are stretched over a sound board and plucked, then this physical metaphor (so to speak) ensues:

As the length is to the length,
So the heard tone is to the heard tone.

Moreover, the pairs of strings producing "tones" (*tonos*; "pitch from tension") that agree—sounds that are agreeable when heard together and are, as we say, "con-sonant"—have to each other the "ratio" of a small whole number to a small whole number. For example, take the simplest and most remarkable case, in which the consonance is a near-identity, the octave. As a string of unit length 2 is to a string of unit length 1, so is the tone an octave below to that an octave above. In other words, if you double the string you get a lower note— the whole scale below. This is the most "agreeable" consonance (because it is a near-identity), though maybe not the most interesting to the ear. But to thought it is fascinating: You've gone across all the tone qualities that a (diatonic) scale includes, say, C, D, E . . . , and reached—a tonal unison with a maximum pitch difference. All the tones of this scale are produced (not, to be sure, in order of pitch) by certain operations on ratios. I will spare the reader the details and say only that when all the tones are all filled in, the result, the complete octave, is what the Pythagoreans called a *harmonia*. *Harmonia* means literally a fitted whole, a piece of mathematico-physical joinery. Its pitch limits, those of the octave, are even now called by the Greek term *diapason*, "through all." That, as it happens, is Heraclitus's descriptive phrase for the wise Design that steers all things "through all (*dia panton*)" (41)!

A series of musical scales is a good example of, and therefore a fine figure for, a certain kind of cyclicality, the sort that ascends and descends spirally—goes through the same pitch positions in the cycle, but rises vertically higher or falls lower.

Three wonders appeared in the Pythagorean discovery: What no doubt excited the Pythagoreans first was the wonderful fact of the small whole-number ratios between strings producing consonant tones. Then there was that even more wonderful fact that the octave, the whole scale of distinct tones (distinguished by their discreteness from the continuity of speech-sounds and the chaos of noise), could be produced by the mathematical operation of "compounding" (see below). But what drove them eventually to derive a philosophical ontology (an account of the being of things) from music was the most wonderful, indeed, the wondrous fact that number ratios, which are the result of measuring and are precisely articulable, are somehow the "same" as the sound qualities of the paired tones. You can express these sensually delight-giving audible events as bare rational items, as pairs of numbers, measured string-lengths or later, frequencies: The deliverances of our senses are expressible through the *logoi* of our minds.

But the moment comes when those rational *logoi* must be more explicitly related to the original sensory events. And now it turns out that to these so moving experiences no precise description attaches; in fact, the most earnest theoreticians, attempting to express even in the most general way the sensual consonance-quality, fall back on similes from other senses, and "sweet" occurs on every third page of their treatises. The Pythagoreans resolved this dilemma by their difficult doctrine that the sense-world *was* numerical and was *constituted* of numbers and number-relations. This meant that in the analogy they had discovered, namely that sounds are to each other as numbers, the numbers were what was really present and the sounds were epi-phenomena, mere incidental sense-effects. I will claim below that Heraclitus thought about this Pythagorean problem in these terms: "What is it in the world's constitutive elements that makes them capable of having quantitative relations?" His answer will be: Fire; the explication will follow (Section III M).

I have called what the Pythagoreans discovered an analogy. That is the literal Greek mathematical term: *analogia*. It means that one and the same *ratio-relation*, for which the Pythagoreans borrowed the term *logos*, was carried up and over (*ana*) the whole expression, a collection of *logoi*. We use the Latin term "proportion," which is in a certain respect more precise, because it indicates that a measured, part-for-part or portion-for-portion relation (*pro-portio*) is involved.

In the symbolism introduced in 1676, here is a proportion:

2:1::8:4::16:8, etc.
(read "2 is to 1 as 8 is to 4 as 16 is to 8," etc.[7])

I will enter here, for future reference, two more examples:

1:2::2:4::4:8 etc.,

in which the terms of the ratios are continuous, and

A:B::B:A,

which looks silly but can be true, though only if the two terms are equal. Below I will liken to it one of Heraclitus's favorite figures, chiasmus, the rhetorical inversion which identifies all terms with each other:

a   b   b   a

Out of everything one and out of one everything. (10)

To return to actual Pythagorean consonances: the most active in the operation of compounding by which the scale is constructed are the *logoi* of the perfect fifth (3:2) and the fourth (4:3). Compounding, though utterly different in meaning, is most easily understood by its modern analogue, multiplication; ratios can't be multiplied since they aren't numbers, but they can be reinterpreted as so-called rational numbers, which include fractions. (In fact, it was Leibniz who appropriated the colon for the notation of division, thus smoothing the transition from a:b to a/b, which signifies a *number* obtained by dividing b into a.) Then $3/2 \times 4/3 = 4/2 = 2$, and the two consonances "compounded" have, in fact, produced the octave, for example, from E above down to A (5 tones), and on down from A to E below (4 tones). Now here, seeing the compounding of ratios translated into notes on a keyboard, the wonder of this operation shows up: What is in mathematics a compounding of *relations* (for ratios are relations), is to the ear much more like an addition of *tones*. Calculating and sensing have parted company. If Heraclitus had taken that in, he must have welcomed it avidly.

The constituents of a proportion are ratios, *logoi*, and the time has come to ask: What is this relation for which the Pythagoreans appropriated the word *logos*, making it into a technical term, and which the Romans translated as *ratio*? Each word denotes "speech" in its own language. I have assumed that for the Pythagoreans a ratio is a relation all numbers can have toward each other. And so they do say:

Logos belongs to all numbers toward each other.
(Diels, p. 451, l. 24)

Also, many terms may enter into one and the same *logos*, such as 2:1, 4:2, 8:4, etc. and their inverses, 1:2, 2:4, 4:8, etc. That is after all what produces a proportion. The *logos*-relation has a name which is *not* a number, here double and half, respectively. Therefore two *logoi* are not properly called "equal" but "*same*." (When the terms collapse into one number and the relation-name transmogrifies into a number-name, a "fraction," a new era in the conception of number, begins—a long, complex, and very significant tale.[8])

So now the *logos* is fixed as a relation, and the great question arises: What sort of relation?

F. The New *logos*

The general theory of the proportion constituted of ratios is set out by Euclid in the fifth book of his *Elements*.[9] "General theory" here means one that includes magnitudes other than numbers, namely geometric ones, among them those that are incommensurable, that have no common measure articulable in natural numbers, and are thus numerically "unspeakable," in Latin, "irrational."[10] It is interesting that Euclid kept separate the special theory of magnitudes that do have to one another the ratio of a (natural) number to a number and that he placed it *later* in the *Elements* (bk. 7), although this was the Pythagorean theory that was antecedent in time, if not in concept. Perhaps he did this because it was rich in itself, or because it was so felicitously related to the physics of music and appealed to the music theorist in him, for he wrote on the mathematical construction of the audible scale; we do not know.

At any rate, the definition of the *logos* that enters into a proportion is given in the general theory:

A ratio (*logos*) is a sort of relation (*schesis*) with respect to size of two magnitudes of the same kind. (Bk. 5, def. 3)

The definition is *prescriptive* in that only *magnitudes* and only those of the *same kind* may enter into the *logos*-relation: straight lines with straight lines, planes with planes, numbers with numbers, and, as he well knew, sounds with sounds—*if* sounds have some measurable aspect *within* them.

That this definition is indeed a postulate rather than a mere observation can be seen in hindsight. Consider the modern conception of velocity in physics: s/t, a rational number, which is a composite of dimensions *different* in kind. But what, on the face of it, can it mean to divide space by time? Yet we do it. It is the very problem whose consideration I am attributing to Heraclitus, and to him first. For the Pythagorean's number-ontology seems to have post-dated him.

The definition is, secondly, *existential* insofar as a *relation* is supposed to exist. The Greek word comes from the verb *echein*, "to have, to hold"; this suggests the English version "habitude," habitual behavior, but it is too strange. The German word *Verhältnis*, which is said, for instance, of the "relationship" lovers maintain, happens to be exactly right. At any rate, the magnitudes are in fact somehow being held together.

And finally, the definition is *evasive* concerning the *nature* of this relationship; it is "a sort of" relation. Another definition (5) will say, once again, not what the relation *is*, but how you *operate* on its terms to make it reveal its quantitative aspects.

I am, of course, not claiming that so advanced a notion of *logos*—advanced, that is, in explicitness—was devised by Pythagoras or known to Heraclitus, but I am thinking that everything in Euclid's definition implicitly there for a post-Pythagorean user of the term was indeed, as we say, "intuitively" present to Heraclitus.

G. The Ratio-Relation

This new *logos* is, then, above all a *relation*. It bonds two terms without merging them. The merger occurs as a definitive break with antique mathematical sensibilities, when, as I've said, the two natural number terms go into one to become a rational, that is, a ratio-number, a fraction, improper or proper. Thus the ratio 2:1, the multiple called double, becomes 2/1, and the inverse ratio 1:2, a submultiple called half, becomes ½, a fraction.

The modern colon-like symbol expresses the ratio-bond; it keeps the terms apart *and* jams them together, as it will come to mark the division of antecedent by consequent. Also, by yet another serendipity, the colon is the symbol which we use to mark direct speech or an apposite thought. Thus it expresses the kind of bonding-over-distance that the *logos*—after all the word for speech—performs: the terms address each other, or better, the antecedent (in Greek, the "leading" term) addresses the consequent (in Greek, the "following" term), which responds with something within itself. In an *analogia*, a proportion, which is a collection of same ratios, all the pairs can be said to "say the same," *homo-logein*, which is the response to *the* Logos Heraclitus requires from all human beings having *logos*, a thinking-and-speaking capacity. Thus the ratio-relation both is and isn't like the metaphor-relation. "As the stars are twinkling in the sky, so the fires are sparkling in the plain": The similarity of the metaphor to the proportion is in the sameness of the bare situation, the multitude of spread-out scintillating objects. The difference is in the fact that the spoken verbs in all their qualitative distinctions (such as "are twinkling" and "are sparkling") are reduced to a symbol—not even the word "is to" is needed, and that is because the relation is not qualitative; not only don't numbers twinkle and sparkle at each other as stars do in their sky or fires in their plain, but they have no times, while stars and fires are very different in their duration. Recall here that in this spirit Heraclitus is given to omitting the copula in his sayings—"One : Everything."

Then where does the mutual responsiveness of number pairs lie? I have said above: "within." But that is *the* question: Is the ratio-relation intrinsic or extrinsic? Is it entirely the epiphenomenon, the secondary appearance, of the character of the terms, produced by the two-ness of 2 and the unit-nature of 1? Or is the *logos* itself responsible for the bonding? Such a loading of potency onto the relation is familiar to our contemporary sensibility; modern pairs are inclined to speak of "working on their relationship" rather than on its terms themselves. In other words, is the ratio-*logos* a power on its own or entirely emergent from the nature of the terms?

I think that the number-ratio is of the latter sort, the qualitative relation of the former. A ratio of number is *nothing but* the number terms up against each other, and that is what the Latin *pro-portio* indicates: The leading term lays a claim on the following term that causes the latter to distribute, to apportion, itself over the former. So 1 : 2 means "2 distributed over (or dividing) 1," which yields the ratio "one-half." Or in the ratio 2 : 3, 3 is apportioned over 2, so that each of the antecedent units responds to one-third of the consequent and two of them to two-thirds, and that is the ratio's name. You can see why it was a relief to collapse the relation into a new sort of number. Nonetheless, it is hard to understand what a fraction really is, why it has a numerator and a denominator, without regressing to the ratio-relation and its distributive juxtaposition.

When, however, the logos relates qualitatively related terms, it has work of its own to do. The relation cannot be completely contained within the constitution of the terms. Here is where the *logos* not only *extracts* the ratio from the terms but *collects* them to begin with. It first gives a similarity-recognizing account that brings together different elements and only then extracts their qualitative relation—as Heraclitus does when he speaks of himself as "dividing each thing according to nature and declaring its relation [to others] (*hokos echei*)" (1). I am taking advantage here of the fact that Heraclitus introduces the activity of "dividing" (*diaireon*), the forerunner of the Platonic "method of division" (*diairesis*), and its dialectical complement "collection" (*synagoge*, *Phaedrus* 266b).

H. The Heraclitean Application

I think that Heraclitus surreptitiously, antagonistically, absorbed something crucial from the reviled Pythagoras, be it man or school—that new meaning for the word *logos*: "relation." It is a sense subordinate to and yet inherent in the great Logos, the Saying whose sentence collects the world into a universal unity and expresses it to those who give heed:

hen : panta—One : Everything.

Notice that, curiously, Heraclitus renders this relation as wordlessly as does the modern colon-notation; of course, the colon that appears here between the terms was supplied by me; the Greek text simply juxtaposes them. I conjecture that in pondering what makes the multifarious world one, he began to think about relationality itself and to consider that a Logos might fill the bill who was all at once the relater of all relations, beyond and within them, a maker of the world-order and himself that order, a world-governor, and also the world—a doer, a sayer, and perhaps himself a listener. I say "perhaps" because the fragments, though full of homage, never mention prayer.

This world-order is what Heraclitus calls by its Pythagorean name the *cosmos*. Cosmos, again, means the world seen as well ordered, well fitted together, a thing handsomely arranged, beautified (the meaning still alive in our "cosmetics"—articles of beautification). Thus he speaks of the "most beautiful harmony" (8) of the whole, the

harmony of the cosmos . . . (By 56),

though this *harmonie* (in Ionian dialect $e = a$), the borrowed Pythagorean term for the scale compounded of consonances, will receive an oppositional, a characteristically Heraclitean, interpretation (Section III K). Moreover:

> The unapparent harmony is stronger than the
> apparent one (54),

which means, I think, that non-sensory *logoi* govern
the sensory world. For this cosmos, having as governor Thinking itself, would be fundamentally rational,
here meaning measurable, that is, capable of ratio-relations—though it has its irrational aspects, among them
people "deaf" to the *logos* (34). (The irrational numbers,
in a nice coincidence, used to be called "surds," the "deaf
ones," as opposed to the audible, articulable rationals.[11])
And the cosmos would be full of virtual and real change
to give the world-governor (who was also the world-
maker, once again to anticipate the exposition) plenty
of scope. Here is what made Aristotle count Heraclitus
among the Physicists (*Metaphysics* 984a): It is a sensible,
moving world that the Logos "informs," in the old sense
of providing it with an inner rationale.

Indeed, there is, as I mentioned, a report that Heraclitus's work was called *On Nature*, but then, that was
also said to be the name of Parmenides' poem, and Parmenides denies that motion is even thinkable. On the
one hand, it is the irony of ironies that the philosopher of the Logos should be called so bluntly a physicist among the "Physicists" he despised. To range him
among them does not do justice to his independence—
and, incidentally, casts suspicion on any history of philosophy that presets it as a staged development. On the
other hand, Aristotle has good apparent cause, since to
him Heraclitus appears to be introducing the element

so far missing in the older, Milesian accounts, namely fire.[12] The trouble is that his Fire is nothing like their stuff. It is rather, I hope to show, that pervasive quasi-material that allows all the elements to enter into quantitative ratio-relations with each other, for it renders them measurable (Section III M).

I. The Milesian Predecessors

What world-orders were on offer? What did the three earlier Milesians provide? The texts are even more fragmentary than Heraclitus's own remains. Evidently there were three elements, three basic stuffs from which the other appearing matters were derived by some process: Water (Thales); The Boundless (Anaximander); Air (Anaximenes). These were the proto-elements, sensible but not quite in the way of the stuff we drink, are immersed in, and breathe. They appear to be more like moisture in general, matter in general, gaseousness in general. They are not the ultimate, wholly abstracted material Aristotle calls *hyle*, pure receptivity, for they are both sensed and capable not so much of specification (as is *hyle*) as of transformation.

Thus Thales's Water was called the "most causative," because it was the most readily transformable. Heraclitus, however, abhors moisture for its soddenness, so Water is not a candidate for primacy. Next, Anaximander ascribes to the Boundless a sort of indeterminacy that does make it a forerunner of Aristotle's above-mentioned "material" cause; why, Anaximander asks, if the basic stuff did have definite qualities, would those not prevail over all? What moves this undefined stuff into determinacy is a retributive, punitive principle. Thus things come into real being and are destroyed

> according to what is owed. For they give each other just retribution and penalty for their injustice according to the order of time. (Diels, Anaximander, 1)

Heraclitus must have been put off by the notion of time as an ordering principle (Section III L) and thought absurd this anthropomorphic cosmo-ethics that punished the arrogation of quality by matter. He says:

> To the god all things are beautiful and good and just, but men understand some things as unjust, some as just. (102)

In the cosmos, seen cosmically, there is no cause for retribution.

Finally, Anaximenes says that

> like our soul which rules us in, so breath and air encompasses the whole cosmos. (Diels, Anaximenes, 2)

He speaks of condensation and rarefaction as the supervening principles of alteration. To Heraclitus the cosmos is not to be externally encompassed—certainly not by a gas—but is internally held together; moreover, thick-and-thin are not fit principles of its changes.[13]

J. Heraclitus the First Physicist

I shall claim that title for Heraclitus and claim it for real: He is, as the first physicist of force and matter, and thus as the first modern scientist, closer to us than is Aristotle, for in the face of originality chronology is a leap-froggable irrelevancy. Compared to him, the Milesians were proto-physicists; I have indicated why he scorns the world-orders already proposed by them. Though he does not mention even a one of these three predecessors, he criticizes them all tacitly. I am assuming here—, as seems fair—that, sessile though he was, he was quite as familiar with the opinions of his neighbors in Miletus to the south on the coast of Asia Minor or in Colophon to his north a little inland as he was with those of Pythagoras who had immigrated to Italy. These early Greeks got around much as did Odysseus, the clever predecessor of them all in inquisitiveness, who knew

the cities and minds of many men (*Odyssey*, 1.3),

and so, presumably, news came to Ephesus.

Here, in sum, is my sense of Heraclitus's sense of all the others' deficiency: They introduce anthropomorphically mythical or unfoundedly technical causes of change, which are inexplicably supervenient upon the elements or mysteriously spontaneous within them—

causeless causes. Nor does their material really *underlie* elemental transformations; rather, it is itself transformed. That is because the stuff is picked according to some idiosyncratically preferred observation. In other words, the principles of change are just imaginative names for some observed behavior that has caught the onlooker's attention.

Aristotle will say, as against these materialists, that anything "has a *nature* (*physis*) which has the cause of change or motion within itself" (*Physics* 142b), as opposed to nature being located in a semi-informed mass of *matter.* And he will grapple with the explanation of such self-motion not in fuzzy physico-mythical terms but with philosophical precision.[14] He thinks that, to avoid endless regression, the ultimate mover of all natures must be unmoved—a divinity, it turns out, who causes motion without external action by being the uninvolved destination of the desirous reaching of appetite.

I think that Heraclitus came on the question of change and motion as a proto-problem, and that he, too, needed a divine cause. But unlike Aristotle's *Nous*, his *Logos is*—at least in one of its aspects—involved in motion. His answer to the question, "What might be the non-temporal source of cosmic motion?" will be incompletely determinate, will be ambivalent, will be in suggestive suspension. He probably thought of that irresolution as jibing with the cosmic truth. I want to reiterate that to a latter-day propensity for preferring flat univocity this way appears primitive. But perhaps we should try to regard it instead as primal, as achieving something remarkable: sophisticated depth, the ability to live in a suspension that is not a fuzzily abridged effort but a fully intended finality—the way of people at the origins. Now I might venture a first comparison: Unresolved dualisms are not unknown to physics; for example, light and matter behave either as particles or as waves under different aspects.

Here, to begin with, is Heraclitus on the design of the world:

> Not a single one of those whose *logoi* I have heard has come so far as to recognize that "Wise" is separated from everything. (108)

Even today it is a problem about (though not within) physics whether the cosmos is guided by an intelligent design and, if so, whether that design is itself impersonal, immanent, incarnate intelligence (meaning that the world is self-organizing), or whether it is produced and administered by the intellect of a divinity above it (meaning that the world is a creation). Heraclitus has answered with firm ambivalence: the "Wise"—as I observed, he will refer to it now without, now with the article[15]—is set off from everything. But that's the answer from only one aspect; this Wise Thing is also incarnate in the cosmos (Section III N). Socrates tells of his youthful search for a physicist who employed an intelligent governing principle; he thought he had found him in Anaxagoras, who offered "Mind" (*nous*) but who, it turned out, had lost it on the way; it proved to be nonfunctional within his physics (*Phaedo* 97). Heraclitus was not so heedless. Part of his thinking is devoted to the question, "How does wisdom get to work *in* the world?" and, again, "Is this principle a 'What' or a 'Who'?" Moreover, "Is it a mere relation of relations or does it have its own substance?"

For the *questions* Heraclitus may have been indebted to his predecessors, that is, to the glaring deficiencies of their gallant attempts. But the *answers* are his own, though not quite in the wonted way of the tradition, in which a next thinker responds to the previous one "dialectically," that is, by taking thought-through issue, or directly, by way of blunt denial or derailing elaboration. Heraclitus goes about it in a more off-beat, all-his-own fashion.[16]

The Physicists, as I have presented them, end up with a single-level nature, whose active principle is adventitious. Three centuries later, the Stoics, those sometimes discerning traducers of Heraclitus, saw the difficulty and explicitly located an active and a passive aspect right *within* the world's matter (Section IV).

Heraclitus's world is, on the other hand, double-leveled; it has a *transcendent* aspect. I say "aspect" because that seems to me peculiarly Heraclitean: the defining characteristic of his main term shifts as it is seen from different perspectives. Once again, since I think it is of the essence: This is not an "early" thinker's muddle begging to be de-confused, but a very unconfused way of seeing the real indeterminacies of the cosmos asking to be followed out.

Another such double aspect is in the answer to the question, "Who or what *is* this design-principle?" It has several names besides "Wise" (Section III N), and it both is and is not a "who," a person, a divinity:

> One is the Wise, alone; and it does not want and
> does want to be called Zeus by name. (32)

For the answer to the crucial question "*How* does the governing principle *work*?" Heraclitus is, once again ungratefully, indebted to Pythagoras. I postpone yet another great question, "*What* does it *work in*?" because it seems to me that for Heraclitus its answer follows from the "How?" question. Here, then, is a further consequence of the Pythagorean *logos*-notion as adapted by Heraclitus. Here is how the Logos governs.

K. Contentious Harmony

The great Logos *collects*, discerns, and then brings the things that constitute the world together—in an incomposably unfriendly, indissolubly intimate face-off. Like his model the Oracle, Heraclitus *signifies* this confrontation. He does it by regularly omitting the copula "is," which is what the colon effects in the ratio-symbolism. This is the way the Logos speaks to the heedful listener:

> The god is day : night, winter : summer, war : peace,
> surfeit : famine. (67)

Another series of tightly jammed terms of antagonistic apposition is listed by Hippolytus, a most copious
and apparently reliable source (Section IV). He places it
just before the great Fragment 50: "Listen not to me but
the Logos . . . ," and it describes the constituents of the
cosmos, the All (*to pan*), held together by that Logos:

divisible : indivisible, born : unborn,
mortal : immortal

—after which Hippolytus goes off on his own.

Then, embedded in that fragment, comes the great-
est of all *logoi*, the Superlogos:

One : Everything,

in which scholars have accepted that deforming emendation by inserting some form of the copula "is."

These confronting terms of a ratio have various kinds
of ratio-relations to each other. Some are contraries developing along a time-spectrum (summer : winter); some
are once-and-for-all contradictions (divisible : indivisible); some are—aspectual—oppositions of nature
(mortal : immortal).

They will all enter into what Heraclitus names a
harmonia. It is, recall, a Pythagorean term. But it is not
the neat fitting achieved by compounding ratios of con-
sonant tones. It is instead an ultimately oppositional
cosmic framework, as of rafters, a terminally contentious joining of antitheses (Section III P).

This is the structure of which Heraclitus says:

The unapparent *harmonia* is stronger than the apparent one. (54)

I have here transcribed the Greek word so as to avoid the feel of Keats's "Heard melodies are sweet, but those unheard / Are sweeter," from the "Ode on a Grecian Urn." "Sweet" and Heraclitus don't go together. His harmony is not a musingly soft or image-enchanted melodious wash. It will turn out to be tensely strained within, a system of virtual action and reaction. As I have intimated, this framework is, first, purely formal, immaterial—that is the unheard, the stronger harmony of fitted *logoi*; and second, it is materially embodied tension—that is the sensed, less potent lock of straining bodies. Just so are the Pythagorean musical ratios pure numbers first and then audible sounds, since numbers underlie the sensory appearances. In fact, Heraclitus has an actual lyre in mind as an embodied framework for *harmonia* (51, Section III O). Viewed as a whole structure, it conveys to him contentious tension made visible rather than melting music made audible. But even the single tones produced on each of the lyre's strings convey tension. This is the dynamic quality a tone develops in the vicinity of another when "the one wants to pass beyond itself, the other wants itself."[17] This musicologist's sentence is almost an explanatory rendering of Heraclitus's arresting phrase "lives the death of . . . ," as in "fire lives the death of earth . . ." (76, see below)—the

THE LOGOS OF HERACLITUS

language of self-assertion and self-conservation through antagonistic intimacy.

So here we have high-toned passion produced by quantitative *logoi*. I imagine that Heraclitus himself resonated readily to their most soul-affecting sensible realization—our basic diatonic, eight-tone music.

But whatever be the "logical" type of opposition displayed in these pairs, they are all in that juxtaposition of which the mathematical ratio-relation is the most transparent type. They are thus a version of Pythagorean *logoi*. As if in corroboration, the crucial qualification of a quantitative *logos* set out in Euclid's definition, the restriction "with respect to size," turns up:

> This cosmos, the same for all . . . an everliving fire, kindled in measures (*metra*) and quenched in measures. (30)

L. Elemental Transformations

Heraclitus has chosen fire as the root-element, the first but not the last to do so (Section IV). The flarings-up and dyings-down of this fire have ratios to each other, as announced in Fragment 30 above; they enter into Euclidean "relations with respect to size." Thus mathematical *logoi* go quite literally cosmo-logical. The world-order is realized in *logos*-governed transformations:

> Turns of fire: first sea, and of sea, the half earth, and the half typhoon . . . Earth is poured out as

sea, and it is measured according to the same ratio (*logos*) as it had before it became earth. (31)[18]

Heraclitus is announcing that the great Logos informs all the changes observed in the cosmos, mostly trans- formations, so that these are governed by fixed ratios, *logoi*. The *changes* (by volume, I guess) are:

fire → sea → ½ earth + ½ typhoon (→ fire).

The second part of the fragment tells of one of the *re- turns* that finally complete the cycle of transformation; they are not always in the same order:

Fire lives the death of earth and air lives the death of fire; water lives the death of air, earth of water. (76)

Thus here (leaving the paradoxical phrase "living the death of" for later, Section III S):

earth → fire → air → water → earth.

The *logoi*, however, remain the same, in any order. That makes what is called an *analogia*, a universal propor- tion, true for any pair of the same elements at differ- ent times. At some point in the cyclical transformation, however, all the ratios are inverted, so that the terms of the departure and the return are equalized, and the ra- tios compounded yield unity. I cannot pretend to under- stand how it would have looked in practical detail, but

I do believe that some such notion was what Heraclitus was pursuing.

Here then is, unmistakably though inchoately, a proto-law of conservation of matter over cycles of transformation; when the cycle is completed there must be the same amount of that element as when it began, and since each element can be considered as beginning the cycle, they are all conserved.

However, a more exact approximation to a scientific law, the Law of Fixity of Composition, is formulable. Here is the law, regarded as "one of the fundamental principles of chemistry":

> If one substance is transformed into another, the masses of these two substances always bear a fixed ratio to each other.[19]

This is so nearly what Heraclitus says that his aphoristic cosmology might be regarded as a project for a future chemistry; it is a proto-chemistry, as it were, the project of discovering the actual ratios of substances.

The many proportions that order and unify the world are realized, as I said, over time:

$$\text{earth } (T_1) : \text{fire } (T_1) :: \text{earth } (T_2) : \text{fire } (T_2)$$

and so on forever. Note another one of Heraclitus's ambivalences: Fire occurs *both* as a term among other element-terms *and* as the universal medium: the "turns of fire," of which more in the next section.

There is no reason to think that all the ratios are nearly the same; I would guess—a mere guess—that it takes, by some common measure, a lot more earth to sublimate into bright flame than it takes water to coagulate into clumpy earth, so

earth : fire > water : earth,

which is to be read as saying that the first *logos* is greater than the second, as, say, $3:1 > 2:1$, since triple is greater than double. Indeed, we have already been told that one measure of sea apportions itself over half earth, half hot whirlwind; thus the ratio of water to earth is $2:1$, plus heat.

So the transformation-ratios between two given elements form a proportion over time, and the cosmos contains many such proportions constituted of other such ratios. One might even go so far as to say that by compounding the different element-ratios one can determine the ratio of any element to any other element—though I won't, because I can't imagine Heraclitus doing any such thing.

The whole collection of ratios might well be entitled

Out of everything one and out of one everything. (10)

Everything is in a fixed ratio-relation that the Super-Ratio, the Hyper-Logos, both knows and administers, steering "everything through everything" (41) by means of the Pythagorean *logoi*. In particular, as I said, when *all* the ratio-pairs of transforming elements are compounded over a whole cycle, the result ought to be *unity*. Or again: The atemporal design instills measure in matter, such that the elemental transformations are reciprocal over a temporal cycle; thus the cosmos, *Everything*, holds steady as a unity, *One*.

As I have mentioned, these proportions develop through time. Heraclitus names time not even once in the surviving fragments. I think it was relegated to that large reservation of condemned notions. Here is what he does say:

> Aeon is a child, childishly playing at moving about counters; the kingdom is a child's! (52)

Aeon or Eon, *aion*, means "an epoch, an age." It is surely intended here to work as a pun: *a-ion* can be read as "un-going." The times go nowhere, events are played out capriciously, as a game played by a child that wantonly breaks the rules. I think the child here is the unruly princeling, the play-absorbed son of royal War:

> War is the Father of all things, of all things
> King. (53)

When the kingdom is in the child's hands, the epoch's tension is in remission and the age is discombobulated. When War rules, the transmutations proceed in their various sequences. In other words, Heraclitus looks to change and its rationale rather than to time as the locus of vital order; he thinks, comments a source, that "the cosmos came about not in accordance with time but thoughtful design (*epinoia*)" (Stobaeus in Wheelwright, p.122). And again there is something very modern in this view; I mean the contemporary attempt to eradicate time from physics.[20] Yet he is first in an ancient tradition as well, one that Aristotle will later work out: that time is subordinate to change in being nothing but the counting of its passage (*Physics* 219b); the notion that time has substantiality bedevils modern mentalities.

M. Solvent Fire

Now this question comes to the fore: The pairs in a successive transformation, the terms in physical *logoi*, are sense objects. What in them, does Heraclitus think, makes them quantitatively relatable in all phases—and what makes them transformable to begin with? "How does mere stuff, surely irrationality incarnate, come to have measurability, numerability, rational relatability?" he must have asked himself. Here is a revealing fragment:

> For Fire everything is an exchange (*antamoibe*)
> and Fire for everything, just as for gold, money
> (*chremata*) and for money, gold. (90)

Written as a qualitative proportion, a metaphorical *analogia*:

> Fire : cosmic currency : : gold : human currency

The usual translation of the last phrase of the fragment is "just as for gold, goods and for goods, gold." *Chremata* does, however, also mean minted money; "Money (*chremata*) [makes] the man," says Alcaeus the lyric poet, of Heraclitus's generation (*Lyra Gracca* 1.81).

Coinage had been introduced—a world-organizing event—in nearby Lydia, as Herodotus tells in the *Persian Wars* (1.94). This first coinage employed gold-plus-silver, a fixed-ratio amalgam called *electron*. Hoards of Lydian coins have been found in a temple in Ephesus. Croesus, King of Lydia, who later issued a coinage of his own, had, in fact, attacked Ephesus within the lifetime of Heraclitus's father, Blosson. So Heraclitus was surely familiar with coinage, and it is entirely plausible that a thinker who had cosmic cycles of transformations on his mind should be fascinated by this new, minted money: You took your gold to the mint and received in exchange currency, a circulating medium of standard weight and guaranteed purity—no short weight or adulteration—and the gold was right there, *in* the coins, of which Aristotle pertinently says:

> Coinage (*nomismata*)—indeed a measure (*metron*), as it were—makes [goods] commensurable (*symmetra*) and equalizes them. (*Nicomachean Ethics* 1133b)

Add the fact that fire is the purifying and liquefying element in minting money, and coined gold would be a perfect analogue to a sought-for cosmic medium, which would, inversely, be most suggestive of fire and its *modus operandi*, its "turns *(tropai)*" (31).

Fragment 90 can also be read as a chiasmus, the X-like figure of speech that connects two terms inversely:

Fire for everything as everything for fire.

Recall that such a proportion of inverse *logoi* betokens an identity of the terms, just as gold and gold coins are indeed identical except that the coin is a piece of distinctively shaped gold (to prevent snipping) bearing a device (to signify the issuing authority, such as a lion on Lydian coinage). Thus the chiasmus signifies a notable but little noticed feature of Heraclitean Fire (which I have been capitalizing to signify its primacy). It is in everything all the time—the all-pervasive, everliving implicit medium that sometimes appears as an element on its own. When it is explicit, it has characteristics that are as destructive as they are beautiful, as reductively disintegrating as leapingly illuminating: "neediness and surfeit" (W 30); it yields now vapor and arid ashes, now light and enlivening warmth—furious consumption ending in sudden satiety.

Moreover, this Fire has marks of intelligence. Hippolytus reports Heraclitus as saying:

Fire is thoughtful *(phronimos)* and causal in the management of all the whole. (Wheelwright, p. 122)

Perhaps it *is* intelligence (Section III N).

Heraclitus therefore takes care that in the aphoristic proportion fire is the leading term, as before he had prefaced his transformations with "the turns of Fire: . . ." (31). But then, in the chiasmus, "everything" gets to lead. For, while to Fire belongs the dignity of governing "everything" *invisibly*, "everything" is what presents itself to us day by day, *visibly*.

Here in summary are the various putative paths by which Heraclitus came to Fire as the element of elements. The borrowing route might have led from Heraclitus's Asian home to the conquering Persians' veneration for fire in its purity; Zoroaster, who introduced fire worship to them, was the Ephesian's contemporary. The low road possibly began in opposition to his rejected teacher Xenophanes, who had said that everything is from, and ends in, earth (Diels, p. 27). A more philosophical point of departure is given by Aristotle, who calls fire the most "kinetic," that is, the most mobile, the most agile element. Heraclitus's most personal motive is his hatred of all things soggy and sodden, his preference for dryness:

The dry soul is the wisest and best (118),

since drunk souls are soggy (117); it is at once delight and death for souls to become wet (77), for wetness betokens somatic abandon. I imagine that Heraclitus thought of dryness, the effect of fire, as making for dignified reserve and "caustic" wit. But of course the highest reason for adopting fire was its luminous discernment, its "analytic," literally its dis-solving, power. Fire, then, as the vitally warming, shiningly illuminating, analytically decomposing, upwardly mobile element, is the cause of measurability. Aristotle mentions a mental constituent, a "matter of mathematicals (*ton mathematikon hyle*)" (*Metaphysics* 1059b16); Heraclitus's physical prototype is Fire, a cosmos-constituting, measure-imparting matter.

But is this Heraclitean fire a metaphorical or a real constituent of the cosmos? I think it is a fire that is real enough in the world so as to hurt and heal. But once again, there is also a Fire behind the scenes, like the "unapparent harmony." There are *two* fires—another case of Heraclitean double-thinking. Here is a pertinent fragment, already cited:

> This world-order (*kosmos*), the same for everything, was made neither by any one of the gods nor of men, but ever was and is and will be: an everliving Fire, kindled in measures and extinguished in measures. (30)

And one more:

> Coming upon everything, the Fire will discriminate (also, "judge") and take down (also, "condemn") everything. (66)

This everliving, measuring, judging Fire is surely not the sensed element, but neither is it a merely metaphorical notion, except in Aristotle's exact sense—that metaphor, in accordance with its literal meaning, "transfer," occurs, among other things, when a name is transferred "from a species to a genus" (*Poetics* 1457b). The general Fire is, however, not a piece of poetry but of philosophy: Heraclitus's vividly concrete way of speaking about that terminally indeterminate element whose innermost defining feature is measure-proneness. Put it this way: Fire is that doppelgänger-like matter in the elements which makes them fungible, commensurable with each other, hence possessed of measure.

Here then is a summary of the various functions fire performs for Heraclitus: Visible fire appears on the scene flaring up and dying down by the same measures as govern all elemental transformations. But there is a Fire that never goes out, being ever-present throughout the cosmos. Its all-penetrating, discriminating nature makes it the medium of choice for cosmic exchanges. Its propensity for taking apart, judging—I interpret: for measuring—imports measurableness to everything; its capacity for taking down, condemning—I interpret: for destruction—sponsors change in everything. It *is* the quantifiability of all physical things, their mathematical second nature as well as their transformability, their capacity for elemental mutation. Fire enables the Logos to inform the cosmos with the most determinate relationality thinkable, that expressed in number-ratios.

So this behind-the-scenes Fire is the first answer to a question first posed by Heraclitus and still very much alive: "What is it about our sensed world that makes it subject to measure and so to mathematics?" What, for example, is behind the relation of the temperature we read off our thermometers to the warmth we feel, or the I.Q. kept in our files to the thoughts we are able to think?"

In concluding this section, I want to go so far as to make a probably unexpected comparison—between this Fire of Heraclitus and the Extension of Descartes, the philosophical founder of modern mathematical physics. As Fire remains everliving in Everything through its transformations and relates all things by making them measurable, so Extension is the primary, pervasive property of all body, and each delimited body is, as *res extensa*, a "thing stretched out"—not a being *in* or *over* space, but a spatial substance, a being *of* space. From its spatiality it derives its measurability—as the elements do from Fire. And as enlivening, moving Fire is inherently dynamic because it is a mode of the divine Logos, so each space-body is aboriginally endowed with motion by God (*Rules for the Direction of the Mind*, written c. 1628, Rule 14; also *Principles of Philosophy*, 1644, pt. 2, para. 36).

So Fire governs from within—as *one* aspect of world-governing. Four more such ruling functions, all collected in the Logos, are to follow.

N. The Multiform Logos

I will try to show that the Logos is, in some aspect, all of these: Fire, God, the Wise, the Common, War. My means, more suggestive than stringent, will be to establish a concatenation of aphorisms. First, the uncreated cosmos "ever was and is and will be ever-living Fire . . ." (31).

Next a fragment quoted above begins: "The god is: . . ." and then goes on to say "satiety and famine" (67); these are pretty nearly the terms used in reverse of fire just now: "neediness and surfeit" (W 30), but so far these are mere hints. Next:

> The lightning bolt (*keraunos*) steers everything. (64)

The *keraunos*, the thunderbolt always represented by a flash of lightning, belongs to Zeus; he hurls it as weapon and wields it as scepter (Figure 4). Only Athena, the Wise Goddess, knows the key to its keep, as Aeschylus tells in the *Eumenides* (l. 827). By *keraunos* Heraclitus means "the eternal fire," says Hippolytus in D 64. As mentioned above, he also reports that Heraclitus calls fire "thoughtful" (or "practically wise," *phronimon*) and responsible for the "management" (*dioikeseos*) of "the whole."[21] But a fragment already cited says:

> The one and only Wise, does not want and does want to be called by the name of Zeus (32),

with a hint that the Wise would prefer, in the first instance, not to be particularized by that anthropomorphic god's name. There is but "one thing" which knows and is the plan of the cosmos and which becomes the wisdom of those who listen to the Logos—

Figure 4. Zeus hurling thunderbolt.

the Wise: to know the design by which everything is steered through everything. (41)

Further, upon listening to the Logos all will agree:

"Wise" is : One/Everything. (50)

Thus they—we—are bidden to say what the Logos is and what it says. Moreover, there is something additional and crucial:

The Wise is separated from everything. (108)

It *is* and it *transcends* nature.

As for the Logos, it is "common" (2); indeed it is, "common and divine," and so also is War (80). War and Zeus are, in turn, "the same thing."[22] Something has already been said, and more is to come below, of "Common," a significant term for Heraclitus, and also of War, Father and King of Everything (Section III S). And finally, to come full circle, this Cosmos, which "ever was and is and will be" is—"everliving Fire" (30).

I think that this linking of identifications means that the impersonal Logos, the general Fire, the fire-wielding God, the designing Wise, the salient Common, and the kingly War are all one and are finally one even with the Cosmos itself. From the human side they are distinguishable as aspects of, as perspectives on, the Logos. From the cosmic side they are differentiated by diverse functions. From the divine view (Heraclitus's) they are immanent and transcendent—both.

Thus Fire, as the pervasive discerning and measure-imparting medium, works immanently like a proto-matter; the Wise, as the plan of the Logos, operates through everything but as its design rather than its constituent; as Zeus's lightning, the ruling function of Fire comes to the fore as a destroying and enlivening force that marshals the transformational phases of the elements; as the Common, the Logos presents itself to the human understanding; as War, it is the tensed vitality of the whole; as Cosmos, it is the collection achieved by the Logos when, through its *logoi* working within, it *does* from beyond what it *says* to us—"One : Everything." In this ring of aspects, Logos and Fire are preeminent. One might say that the Logos proposes "audibly" and the Fire disposes "visibly."

A critic might certainly be tempted to regard Heraclitus's gyre of notions as a merry-go-round in want of some uncompromising logical halt-calling.[23] The concatenation of terms I have set out in this subsection isn't even the worst of it; that comes when his paradoxes and contradictions are to be considered (Section III R). Yet I wonder if Heraclitus's Logos wouldn't be a victim rather than a beneficiary of the rectifying *furor logicus*. It isn't that formal logic had not yet been invented in the late sixth century B.C.E., so that people couldn't fairly be expected to think straight. It is rather that his Logos might be timelessly unamenable to law-decreed logic, and that what seems to us, with respect to thought, a case of "not yet" on Heraclitus's side, is really a case of "no longer" on ours. I am thinking primarily of the Law of Contradiction, whose implicit breaching is easily exposed by a bald side-by-side display of conflicting statements. His darkly oracular sayings, on the other hand, are less straightforwardly shown up for falsity, because first you have to extract a plain meaning upon which to work the logic. Here is an example that combines both aspects, contradictoriness and oracularity: The cosmos that is always, is an ever-living Fire kindled and quenched by measures. How can the cosmos be a fire when we know it to contain earth, water, and whirlwinds? And how can it be both everlasting and go on and off? It can't be and do all this unless you concede the double nature of fire, as *being* one element among elements and as *acting* like a principle through them all. In fact, Aristotle actually calls fire Heraclitus's "ruling principle (*arche*)" (*Physics* 984a). As for being both everlasting and going in and also out of being—of which alternation his ever-traducing heirs, the Stoics (Section IV), made a periodic conflagration (*ekpyrosis*)—one solution is that these flare-ups are merely local.

The more general answer to Heraclitus's paradoxicality is that he meant to give the account (*logos*) of the world in its own cosmic terms, not in those of the merely human "logical" laws of thought. I would say that the self-consciously proud production of so many contradictions attests to a great sensitivity to ordinary orthodox thinking. Heraclitus, who told his fellow-Ephesians to go hang themselves (121), tried to think from the god's perspective under which apparently incomposable inner-cosmic antitheses disappear; once again:

> To the god all things are beautiful and good and just, but men have understood some things as unjust, some as just. (102)

Viewed locally, the cosmos looks cloven, and the negative appears first; viewed comprehensively it comes together as a true cosmos: everything tensely bonded but not melded. Heraclitus finds that beautiful and right.

O. The Qualitative Metaphor

So far I have been dealing with the *logoi* governing elemental temporal transformations, which are, by Heraclitus's own testimony, quantitative and, moreover, numerical. These *logoi* are, I have speculated, under the management of the Logos and are perhaps the expressions of "his" Wisdom. Working in the cosmos, the Logos steers everything through everything and thus relates everything in a unity. Speaking to us, it extracts the measures from the fired-up elements, collects them as terms in *logoi*, in ratios, and imparts the result to those who can hear.

Heraclitus, however, speaks also of qualitative relations, often in metaphors. Now a mathematical *analogia* is totally transparent because all its *logoi*, its ratios, are the same and arise out of terms that are the same in kind.[24] The metaphorical analogy is richer, hence more complex. Its terms are not the same in kind in any meaningful sense, for the *logoi* of a metaphor are sentence-like, so that the antecedent is a grammatical subject and the consequent the predicate. Moreover the relations brought together in the analogy are not the *same* but are rather *similar*. Similarity or likeness, that is to say, sameness with difference, turns out to be a great future issue, particularly as it grounds images; the leading text is Plato's *Sophist* (240).

A metaphor, as any poetry handbook will tell, consists of a subject (also called the "tenor") and a figure (or "vehicle"). In our Homeric metaphor, the subject is the Trojan plain; the figure is the stars in the sky: The plain of Troy is like the stars in the sky. This figure throws an expansive background behind, or a novel light on, the subject. It couldn't effect that if the internal relations of the figure (as set out in the sentence "The stars sparkle in the sky") were the same rather than merely similar to those of the subject (as set out in the sentence "The Trojan fires burn in the plain"). For example, the stars spread over the sky sparkle eternally, but the Trojan campfires burn just that night, and many of the warriors sleeping by them will be dead by the next evening. Therein lies the metaphor's pathos, as well as the art of finding figures: they must be like enough to be near-congruent with the subject and different enough to illumine it. Like Homer, Heraclitus is a master of metaphorical speech. But where Homeric metaphors are often consoling, putting scenes of domesticity behind the work of warfare and of natural power behind human violence, Heraclitean aphorisms are meant to be unsettling—very unsettling. In fact, Heraclitus chides Homer for his pacific hopes, in that

> he would abolish strife from among both gods and men. For then everything would be done for. (W 27)

Heraclitus's qualitative *logoi* do not relate terms in friendly mutual address but in antagonistic opposition. Indeed the ratio-relation can be regarded as primarily holding these terms apart rather than together, just as rafters lean into each other to spread the wings of a sloping roof. Recall that collapsing the ratio of two terms into a single rational number, a fraction, was a late and daring step in the expansive unification of the number system.

Here is a typical fragment, first quoted in Heraclitus's terse language, then written so as to display the metaphor implicit in it: Speaking of the cosmos, he says that people don't understand how

> differing it agrees with itself: back-tensed tuning (*palintonos harmonia*), just as of bow and lyre (51; reading *palintonos* rather than *palintropos* because the former refers to "toned," that is "tuned by tensing," which fits the musical term "harmony" better than the latter, "back-turned")

—and, indeed, people don't. The "belch-battling" doctor Eryximachus, who speaks in Plato's *Symposium*, quoting a—mauled—version of this fragment, just can't understand how Heraclitus could commit so great an absurdity as to speak of harmony as difference: "For harmony is consonance" (187b). Period. It is the signature of a collapse-prone mind.

Here is the same fragment rewritten as a metaphor:

Difference and agreement are to the cosmic *harmo-nia* as a back-tensed tuning is to a bow and lyre,

where "tuning" is the translation of *harmonia* when applied to the tuned stringing of instruments. The figure signifies that the cosmos is vibrantly tensed by the same strained bond that sets a bow or lyre twanging. Heraclitus is all for a high-strung world. One more:

Encounters: Wholes and not Wholes, what agrees and disagrees, is consonant and dissonant, and out of everything one and out of one everything. (10)

Aristotle quotes this passage in *On the World* (396b), ascribing it to "Heraclitus, called the Obscure." And indeed, Aristotle doesn't get it; he cites it in connection with the mixing of colors, the union of tones in a harmony (evidently in our sense of chordal consonances), and the blending of mutes and vowels. He speaks of the like-mindedness (*homonoia*) of pairs of opposites, such as males and females. These are unitings by meldings. But that is just what Heraclitus, the plain and radical, *doesn't* mean. Oppositions do not compose in sweetness and light. It's war, not peace, that maintains a taut and fiery cosmos.

P. Oppositional Pairs

Now some answers to the question "How are Heraclitean pairs actually related?" can be attempted. Elements have quantitative ratios to each other, fixed by the Logos's design and imparted by its fiery operations, which, mediated by a pervasive rationalizing material—hence both as acting *on* and as being *in* the elements—apportions them to each other, so that orderly, proportionate transformations can occur. Thus qualitatively different stuffs can co-respond to each other.

But there are also intensely related pairs that are not of like kind in being fire-based stuff, but are starkly opposed in logical opposition. They are of two logical types (though I do not think Heraclitus did so distinguish them). There are juxtapositions of quality—connected *contraries*, antitheses both separated and held together by a whole spectrum in between, like the surfeit-and-famine attributed both to god and fire (67, 63), which are mediated by degrees of sufficiency or dearth. Then there are abrupt, unmediated confrontations of *contradictories* "wholes and not-wholes," said of all kinds of "encounters" (10).

The Logos can collect these opposites into pairs only by force, not by instilling in and extracting from the terms themselves the ratio-responses. These encounters have nothing but their antagonisms to hold them together in a tight relation, a condition which comes out, curiously enough, in the fact that when you remove the negative, in itself a mere nothing, they collapse into a unity: "wholes and wholes."

Hence here the relation assumes a substance of its own. I mean that a *logos* does not just read off the numbers by which the elemental pairs are measured, but has, or rather *is*, a force in itself.

That makes more plausible the ancient name *On Nature* attached to Heraclitus's composition. It *was* about nature in the sense of treating kinds of matter and causes of motion. It differs, however, from every other early *physiologia* or "account of nature," including Aristotle's *Physics*, in being astoundingly forward-looking, comparable neither to the Presocratics' competitively idiosyncratic choice of an underlying matter which is moved by mytho-physical principles, nor to Aristotle's thing-based physics, in which each natural being has its source of motion within and its purposive cause without, tending ultimately toward a final cause of all motion that is itself beyond all motion. Compared (chronology aside) with Aristotle's science, Heraclitus's physics does indeed look like a rudimentary but real project for the kind of scientific inquiry respected in modernity: a matter-based mathematical physics, where fire functions as potentiality, transformation replaces actualization, and formal cause (design) supplants final cause (fulfillment). And as number-*logoi*, ratios, are the forerunners of rational numbers, so *analogiai*, proportions, are the avatars of equations.

Moreover, Heraclitus himself was greatly sense-oriented, provided the observations were carried on under the aegis of *logos*, both human and supra-human. He says:

[O]f what there is sight, hearing, learning (*mathesis*)—these I honor especially. (55)

Though, on the other hand:

> Bad witnesses to men are the eyes and ears of those
> who have barbarian souls. (107)

Here "barbarian souls" aren't, I think, the souls of boors who lack civilization or of foreigners whose utterance sounds like bar-bar-bar; they are rather the speechless souls of those who are incapable of hearing and agreeing with the Logos and of employing *logoi*, rational expressions, to convey what they have witnessed—in Greek, to be sure.

Moreover, he thinks that

> the eyes are more accurate witnesses than the
> ears (101a),

which I understand to hold only of sensory learning. For example, the cosmic Fire does become visible to observant eyes as fire. The ears have nothing similar to discern, for the Logos, though "heard," is not audible to the ears but to the soul.—Heraclitus is forgetting, or perhaps rather suppressing, Pythagorean music.

It appears that Heraclitus does not feel bound by the—possibly later—rule that the terms of a ratio must be "of the same kind," and that too is a touch of modernity in him. Even Galileo still felt constrained by the rule of homogeneity, so that he never permitted himself to write "s/t," that is, space related to time, the ratio that defines velocity. However, once ratios are collapsed into rational numbers, the rule becomes moot. Thereafter s/t—read "space divided by time" and savor its conceptual absurdity—becomes permissible because it is actually just a "dimension," the numerical terms having shed all sensory qualities and being related to their original concepts merely by a mental dictionary; thus understood, $v = s/t$ is the first defining formula of kinematics.[25] Heraclitus is likewise willing—no, eager—to relate the most diametrically unlike qualities: contradictories. (As it happens, logicians refer to the affirmative or negative form of a proposition as its logical "quality.")

Just to remind the reader, I have already claimed that Heraclitus had a prototype law of conservation of matter—that after the reconstruction of elements, after their cycling through, there is neither more nor less of their volume or mass (to introduce an anachronistic dimension). So also for the fixed ratios of elemental transformations; the relative amounts are always the same.

I now want, hesitantly, to defend him against the charge of unintended ambiguity with respect to the nature of matter: Is his fire essentially matter and materially immersed within matter? Or is it abstracted from sensuous qualities? To me it seems that the *matter* conceived by various kinds of materialist philosophers of science and the *mass* (that is, the measurable aspect of a given portion of matter) operated with by our practicing physicists have a similar *double-entendre* about them: Are they, for instance, meant to be some primary real-world stuff imbued with abstractable sensory qualities like hardness, heaviness, and heat? Or, reversely, are they to be thought of as general matter abstracted from, yet underlying, such qualities? Or are they to be taken as pure mathematical solids imagined into real space? His problematic multivalences survive.

And now to Heraclitus's most remarkable physical notion.

Q. Cosmic Antagonisms

Heraclitus's force-physics is, to be sure, pre-mathematical, but in one particular, at least, it is astoundingly, observantly, intuitive, hence prescient: tension.

Look at the "back-tensed harmony" (*palintonos harmonia*) of the bow and lyre of Fragment 54. Consider either the way the tips of the bow are drawn toward each other by a sinew shorter than the extended bow, or the way the arms of a lyre are pulled together by means of the "yoke" to which are affixed the strings, twisted tight by turning pegs. Ask yourself: "Just *where* is the tension?" In the string, it seems, but just where in it? In the whole of it, surely, insofar as it relates the two tips or the arms, being the connection between them. In fact, if you cut the string of the bow held upright anywhere and attach to the dangling upper end a weight that pulls in the tip just as before, you will find that it is the same for any cut: The tension *on* the string is the same at each of its points. Yet the string itself is a mere conduit of connection; for there is *no* tensile force coming from the tips *in* the uncut string as a whole: The read-out of a spring-balance inserted anywhere *within* the string will be 0. (This string is assumed to be idealized, meaning its stretching is irrelevant to the bending of the tips; it could be a rod.) For each terminal, each tip, pulls back oppositely and equally by a version of Newton's Third Law of Motion, that of Equal Action and Reaction, or rather, by nature's design; again, the string is a neutral conduit. Moreover, if you load two weights on either end of the string hung horizontally over pulleys, substituting the weights for the tips pulled inward, each will reveal the whole force the string asserts, though that does not double the force in the string! Only a physics book for amateurs would deign to notice how strange this in-between force, this tension, is.[26] It is the relating, the in-between, the mediating force-conduit *par excellence*, at every point and through the whole, nothing in itself and everything in its effect—nothing but relation, yet as such all-potent. That is what Heraclitus both observed and intuited: a relation that is quantitatively nothing, but qualitatively everything.

I note here a felicitous fact concerning Newton's Third Law, which might be called the dynamic formulation of Heraclitus's world, both natural and human. When Kant provides the transcendental grounding of what turns out to be this law of equal action and reaction, he heads it as "Grounding Principle of Coexistence According to the Law of Reciprocal Action, or Community" (B 256). In Heraclitean terms, the pervasive mutuality of force is the principle of oneness—of coexistence in a force-community.

Heraclitus introduces such a force to hold the cosmos, "everything" (*panta*), together in a vibrantly antagonistic tension. That is what is expressed in the super-chiasmus: "Out of everything one and out of one everything." This is what the Logos utters, inaudibly but heedably, in its capacity as the design-making Wise (10, 50). Everything is held together by the unity of opposites, but *not* as their reconciliation, *not* in a Homeric spirit of regret for strife, or in a Pythagorean harmony of consonances. For then, Heraclitus says, "everything" would "be done for," "go by the board," "go off and away" (*oichesesthai panta*) (W 27).

Of course, I am not claiming that Heraclitus had devised an early modern dynamics with a well-defined notion of force. For one thing, there seems to be no thought of acceleration, which is the first and decisive modern elaboration on velocity (as we say, a *second* derivative, the rate of change of change). What I do mean is that he had a heeding intuition for the relations of strenuous togetherness, of strained union, a relation that now degrades and then again vitalizes a world as a multiplicity that can present itself to us as an ordered whole—a cosmos.

This Heraclitean tension between opposites in space or time or quality is, it seems to me, the ultimate substantial, *qualitative* relation. For opposites are identical except for the unbridgeable gulf of mutual negation, and therefore cannot, as it were, "address" each other except through their antagonism. Tension is the relation of antithetical sameness. (Recall again that later logicians will term the positive or negative character of a *logos* its "logical quality.")

There is a lovely, archaic, shallow-carved relief cut on the base of a (missing) statue in the National Museum at Athens.[27] (Figure 5. "Archaic" is a term in art history referring to pre-classical works; thus it is, one might say, the counterpart to "Presocratic" in philosophy.) As it happens, it was made during Heraclitus's lifetime. It is a gymnasium scene—"gymnasium" is Greek for a place of "naked training"—and so the young men are nude as they engage in all sorts of sport. Central, however, are two youths engaged—here the felicitous word—in a wrestling contest; the Greek word for "contest" is—again felicitously—*agonia*: They are painfully but intimately locked in a wrestler's hold. They lean into each other, heads abutting, the hands of one pushing the opponent's right shoulder, the other's pulling his partner's left wrist. It is the very picture of muscle-straining stasis; it is the tension-*logos* incarnate: human rafters, just as Homer describes them (*Iliad* 23.711).

Figure 5. Wrestlers on an archaic base.

In time the mutually bracing lock will break up—
all may fall down—and then they will take a new hold,
entering another cycle of stasis and transformation. The
chiasmus of contradictories such as "immortals: mortals, mortals: immortals" (62), begins to make sense
if either both terms are the same by nature or if they
turn into each other in time. Thus, this favored Heraclitean expression invites both kinds of interpretation: the
ineradicable self-contrarieties of nature at any moment,
and the permissible contradictions of verbally expressed
change over time. Gods may always have some touch
of mortality in their nature and humans may become
immortal in time.

Heraclitus had evidently often observed such bal-
anced "agonies," of antithetical natural forces and
human values, and had found them both exhilarating
and suggestive. It was what others had missed:

> They don't understand how differing from itself it
> stays the same (or agrees, *homologei*) with itself: the
> back-tensed tuning (*palintonos harmonia*), just as of
> bow and lyre. (51, probably came close to Fragment
> 1 in the "Composition," see figures 6 and 7)

Indeed, the very name of musical sound, *tonos*, expresses
tension (from the verb *teinein*, "to stretch tight"). So:

> The hostile: what collects together (or agrees,
> *sympheron*). And from things that differ: the most
> beautiful harmony. And all things come to be from
> strife. (8)

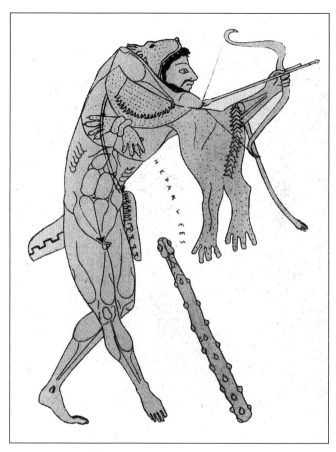

Figure 6. Heracles shooting his bow.

Figure 7. Silenus playing the lyre.

Sympheron also means the "profitable"—the profitably hostile encounter is what Heraclitus has seen in the world.

This "tuning"—one good translation of *harmonia*, insofar as the Pythagorean ratios guided the tuning of stringed instruments—may be beautiful because it is composed basically of consonances, though I wouldn't be surprised if Heraclitus were the first (and perhaps only) Greek actually to enjoy dissonance: the harmony, the joining, not of consonance but of dissonance— a very modern taste. The tensed bow consequently twangs in opposite voices—a joyful and a terrible one; delight-giving and death-dealing at once—as its two names indicate.

> The name given to the bow (*toxon*) is *biós*, but its work is death. (48)

Biós, a second word for bow, is nearly homonymous with *bíos*, the word for life (as in our "biology"; our word for "toxic" comes from the poisoned arrow tips issuing from the bow). The vital antagonism, bracing in one way, can be very unfriendly in another. As so often, a homonym—one sound, two senses—expresses Heraclitus's intuition.

Behind all the tensed tunings and strained fittings that appear as sensed *logoi* is the governing Logos's invisible Wise Design, which is audible only to the mind. This wise rationale is the unapparent harmony that is stronger than the apparent one (54). For "nature loves to hide itself" (123). Here "nature" means, I think, what is revealed in *physiologia*, the account of *logoi*-directed motion and tensed stasis that is realized in the sensibles of the sensory world but works behind them, concealed but audible, though only to human *logos*, to thinking.

I cannot resist concluding this subsection with a risky observation—that Heraclitus *sees* his divinity, the Wisdom that wants and does not want to be called Zeus, in appearances and *thinks* him through his wise Design, his structure, and that in this he is appreciably like his proper successors, Galileo and Newton, the founders respectively of kinematics and dynamics, and thus of modern physics. This is from the General Scholium, added by Newton in 1713 to the second edition of his *Philosophiae Naturalis Principia Mathematica*:

> We know [God] only . . . by his most wise and best designs (*structuras*) of things . . . [He] is said to see, to hear, to speak . . . by allegory . . . For all talk of God is appropriated from human affairs by a certain similitude . . . And so much of God, to discourse of whom from appearances surely belongs to natural philosophy.

R. Sensible Paradoxes

Those infamous Heraclitean paradoxes, which look to logicians like paralogisms, fallacies of reason, are, I think, the expressions precisely adequate to his world-order. The Logos collects and expresses this world's nature in *logoi*. These are the ratio-relations between two terms of pairs that are sometimes in numerical relation, but often in relations of contradiction and contrariety. For the human *logos*, human speech, has a capacity that is both strange and apropos. It can utter heedless contradictions; it can speak in a self-deaf way such as Aristotle is so willing to attribute to Heraclitus, that aboriginal listener to the Logos! He says that Heraclitus speaks "not listening to himself," (*Metaphysics* 1262a)—when no one has ever listened harder to the Logos within!

Aristotle's charge does, however, imply that people need not possess his own formal expression of the Law of (non-) Contradiction to speak in agreement with themselves. Therefore Heraclitus's paradoxes aren't the result of not yet knowing formal logic. So unless he is an "idiot," they are quite intentional. Indeed, I doubt that anyone doubts their malice aforethought, since he uses a self-conscious style to express these offending maxims, these *gnomai*, by which the Wise works: it is, as I have already mentioned, the omission of the copula. We too have such gnomic sentences: "No pain, no gain." This is the speech of abrupt antithesis, whose Heraclitean sum and culmination is—One:Everything (50).

There are, as I have indicated, two kinds of antagonisms. I set out first the destructive release of the elements into transformations, their successive and cyclical coming into and going out of their own being, controlled by fixed ratios and ordered sequences. Add to those the cosmic compulsion that keeps natural bodies in their fixed orbits:

Helios (the sun) will not overstep his measure; [for if
he does] the Furies, the servants of justice, will find
him out. (94)

Here the cosmos is viewed, somewhat in Anaximander's
way, as a moral order of liberties attempted and disci-
pline restored, but that aspect of Heraclitus's worldview
is beyond my present brief.

These sequential contraries, be it, say, air : water (34)
or summer : winter (67), are logically perfectly legitimate
because time annuls the Law of Contradiction: factual
contradiction is time-curable. In fact, one of Aristotle's
statements of the law includes the qualification "at the
same time": "It is not acceptable for the same thing to
be and not to be at one and the same time" (*Metaphysics* 1062a). This form is, of course, the Law of Contradiction for being, not for speaking, but so much the
better for my context, since my point is that Heraclitus
speaks paradoxically because that is *how* the world *is*.
In an earlier formulation, Aristotle had cited some people as supposing Heraclitus to say that the same thing is
and is not. He doesn't in fact say that, at least not in any
fragment we have, other than Aristotle's own report.
But, once again, he saves Heraclitus by driving a wedge
between him and his sayings, appealing for this trick to
our *logos*'s wondrous ability to speak in-credible nonsense: "For it isn't necessary that what a man says, that
he also accepts" (1005b).[28]

So there is nothing logically wrong with contraries or contradictions over time. Indeed "contradiction

through time" is a definition of coming-into-being and of change: Then it was, now it isn't, later it will be—each time-phase brings different or opposing conditions. But once again: Time never appears in the fragments; it is change that does it all. In fact, the only appearance of time is *as* change—a remarkably advanced demythification.

There was, however, a second sort of logical antagonism in my account (Section III Q), not resoluble into natural sequential change. That sort is a static opposition, and its description indeed calls for paradox, the indissolubly simultaneous antithesis that sets the world vitally vibrating. For that is effectively what paradox is: a saying that flies in the face of, that goes against (*para*) received opinion (*doxa*) and which effects that by being logically scandalizing. It takes a high-strung, taut philosophical imagination to envision the world so ambivalently:

> It scatters and again gathers; it attacks and recedes (91),

sometimes both at once.

I don't think that so ultimately uncompromising a philosophical physics ever again comes on the scene. Socrates' post-Heraclitean soul-lyre's invisible tuning yields a blend (*krasis*) (*Phaedo* 85e ff); and to leap over millennia, Nicholas of Cusa (b. 1401), a putative Heraclitean heir since he sees God as a "coincidence of opposites," in fact regards these opposites as *reconciled* in the divinity. And so on to Hegel's "sublations" (Section IV). For Heraclitus's divine Logos rationally collects the terms, yet brutely *keeps* the antagonisms—and imparts them to Heraclitus in its lucid thought-speak for him to express in terse paradoxes of Greek speech.

His is, in its parts *and* as a whole, a tautly vital, twangingly alive, strainingly static cosmos. It is a world unified by confrontational encounters, propped up by mutual antagonisms, locked into inimical embraces. It displays a mode of being that is a harsh, ever-unfulfilled striving, the inverse forerunner of Aristotle's *energeia*, his vibrantly static fulfillment—finalities both, yet how differently achieved!

Hence for Heraclitus self-contradiction is indeed the vital crux of the cosmos, as expressed in his ratio-like juxtapositions and in his supposedly obscurantist paradoxes. Moreover, among paradoxes, one specially prominent type is the bald assertion of the identity of opposites, for example:

> The mutually abrasive [is the] advantageous. (8, here translated literally to sharpen the hostility: *to antixoun* means "what scrapes against each other")

There are indeed hopelessly ineradicable logical paradoxes like that of the Cretan liar—"A Cretan says: 'All Cretans lie'"—and there are willfully witty aphoristic paradoxes—"I can resist everything except temptation." But those of Heraclitus are of neither sort. His are cold sober reports of real cosmic ambivalences, notes from

a bi-valent world. It is a realm constituted of oppositions, now stably locked together in a wrestler's hold,
now suddenly parted in a catastrophic transformation,
as when fighters break apart and gain the distance to
strike home. That is its genesis and its rule:

War is Father of all things, of all things King. (53)

Antagonisms are, once more, ultimate.

Heraclitus can both see a world constituted of
antitheses and enunciate it as orderly because the Logos
not only drives everything apart into confronting terms
that face each other in fixed measures, but it also, and
even primarily, collects everything into a unity:

[1.] Out of everything one and [2.] out of one everything. (10)

Thus the ratio-relations that express the Logos in the
world are at once confrontations and correspondences.

Why is the cosmos oppositional? Because it shows itself that way to an observer like Heraclitus. To be sure.
But, if pressed, could and would he respond with reasons to support the brute fact? In this inquiry, a dan-
ger lurks.

One might respond, being helpful to Heraclitus,
along the following lines, incidentally also suggest-
ing how the Logos came to Heraclitus: Agreed that the
beings within the world look as if they were locked in
opposition—unified paradoxically and yet quite pre-

cisely, by reason of their diversity along a whole spectrum of divergence, from subtle differences to stark antitheses. That occurs, you, Heraclitus, must be thinking, because they are under the governance of the Logos's Design, the incarnation of his Wise Structure. But this Logos is itself designed (be it by Heraclitus or in truth) to design the ordered world, the cosmos, from two principle-aspects.

In one of these aspects, your Logos is a principle speaking the language of elemental nature. It says yes to this and no to that; it affirms and denies. In the language of governance spoken to the real world, this means: "Be preserved! *or* Be Destroyed!" or "Stay *or* Go!"—the Logos orders and tells the measures of these *transformations*. Still in this mode, the Logos sometimes contra-dicts itself, says "Yes *and* No" at once; then its incarnation, especially in the human world, appears as the contest of opponents, both striving to *be at once*.

In the other aspect, the opposite principle goes to work, that of collecting everything into one, of relating all things through an underlying element.

Now this apparently helpful explanation has implicitly undermined Heraclitus's intention. For it has implied that his divine Logos is but an image of that human *logos* whose principal uses were set out above (Section II). A central meaning of this lesser *logos*, the one that positions it between the single word and the whole tale, is that of "sentence." A sentence does indeed have the two capabilities just ascribed to the Logos: First, it can assert or negate, posit or remove, maintain or abrogate in the now or over time—and it can contradict itself by doing both at once. In fact, it is the easiest thing in the world to utter a verbal contradiction, though much harder to entertain a mental one. This is indeed an arresting fact of speech—that what logicians claim you cannot *say*, you can so easily *utter*. And second, the Logos can—indeed this is its chief function—collect and express the collection of multiplicities into unities. That is surely what the subject-predicate structure of a sentence effects: "Everything *is* One."

Would Heraclitus be glad to be told that the governor of the world is modeled on a human sentence? I doubt it. The thought is a scholar's taking-down of a philosopher. As he says:

> Much-learning (*polymathie*; translate for the purpose "scholarliness") does not teach [anyone] to have a mind. (40)

So that reductive explanation must be retracted, though it may survive as a helpful hint for comprehending the Logos. The reason why the world is as it is, or how Heraclitus came to hear the Logos, is unavailable. Heraclitus may have said more that is lost to us, but I doubt that too. I will suggest below that his inherent fragmentariness entails a certain philosophical completeness, that what looks like mere human provisionality may express a true cosmic ultimacy. I might go so far in Heraclitus's behalf as to propose that the difference between a wise human being (*sophos*) and a wisdom-seeking one (*philosophos*) is the willing capacity for the long-term entertainment of paradox, and that no human being *is* actually wise, but there *are* philosophers—though not professional ones.

S. Father War

So it is Cosmic War for Heraclitus:

> War is Father of all things, of all things King. (53)

This chiasmus expresses the equality of the generative and the ordering role of strife. Furthermore:

> It is needful to know that War is Common and Justice [is] strife, and that everything comes to be according to strife and what must be (*chreon*). (80)[29]

Here again War is, like the Logos and the Wise and Fire, identified with the Common to complete the quintet of identifications, Heraclitus will have known Homer's simile, used of warriors, dueling close-up, chest-to-chest:

> They contended like blazing *fire*. (*Iliad* 18.1)

Heraclitus might have heard in that line the cosmic antagonism under its most anthropomorphic aspect. This is not the static tension of the stringed lyre but the mobile clash of living fore-fighters in its terrible splendor, in which punitive damages are exacted and new conditions are born. Thus War is father of hazard-ridden confusion—that's his epoch-child at play with human destinies. And he is king of fiery transformations—those are the life-giving deaths of the elements:

Fire lives the death of earth, and air lives the death of fire, and water lives . . . (76, also 36, 62),

which doesn't, I think, mean anything so flabbily trite as that everything comes to be by consuming something else, but that the death of the strife-coupled partner is enlivening, not by the consumption of an alien matter but by the arrogation of an opposing nature. That holds even for mere elements and certainly for human beings. It is not what Homer felt battle to be since he says what Heraclitus blames him for: "Would that strife might be utterly lost from among gods and men" (W 27). What a revealing reversal of the usual relation of poet and philosopher! Ordinarily the former revels in agonized extremities, the latter calls for the smoothing effect of sweet reason. (Unanswerable query: Was Heraclitus ever a soldier?)

But the philosophically most arresting meaning is this: Fire, at least, is not abolished in the transformations, but rather preserved; each presently existing element has in it the everliving first Fire (Section III M). I will speculate further: Each superseding element must both destroy *and save* (Hegel would say "sublate") the previous element, must absorb something formative in it—else how would it be resurrected and reappear at a cycle's end? Thus each element very pregnantly "lives the other's death."

T. That Flux

These are among the most famous sayings of Heraclitus:

Everything flows, and nothing stays,

and:

Everything gives way and nothing stays. (both W 20)

The trouble is that he never said the first; it is attributed by Plato to "those around him," whose doctrine that everything flows he supplies with the derisory addition "like leaky pots" (*Cratylus* 440c). The second seems to be like a distorting interpretation rather than a quotation. After all, Heraclitus thinks of strife precisely as keeping everything from "going by the board" (W 27). Neither fragment has been accepted into the canon.[30]

Here is another saying, which was evidently really said by Heraclitus:

A river—it is not possible to step into the same one twice. For other and ever other water flows on. (91 combined with 12)

This last aphorism gained notoriety from the fact that Cratylus, whom Aristotle calls a "Heraclitizer" with the "most extreme opinions," added: "not even once" (*Metaphysics* 1010a). Since Heraclitus wasn't a man you could follow, the attempt not merely to follow but to trump him must of necessity have led to hyperbolic nonsense. For since it makes no sense to be able to step into the *same* river once to begin with (since a judgment of sameness needs two tries), what can it mean not to be able to do what is unmeaning? Nonetheless, it's clear what Cratylus was after: the extreme version of radical flux, ultimate inconstancy. For him there is no "*a* river" or, for that matter, anything at all that retains its being.

Is this philosophy of radical flux compatible with the notions of vibrant stasis, of orderly transformations, of a wise Design, a discerning Fire, a governing Logos—of "One: Everything"? Not remotely.

First it has to be acknowledged that both Plato and Aristotle were ready to propagate this Flux-Heraclitus. Heraclitus the Obscure made a good relativistic whipping-boy; thus they are the sources of the fragments just quoted (Section IV).

What does the genuine river-fragment actually say? It begins by acknowledging that there *is* a river, and from its banks one can step into it—not twice, yet also, in good Heraclitean style, twice. For the river is the same and not the same: bed-and-bank stay put, the waters roll on. It is an odd—but perhaps revealing—circumstance that the one time he teeters on the edge of triteness is the time he is memorialized.

Nor is he a relativist, one who believes that things and events are probably not determinate in themselves, and surely not stably determinable, but acquire some passing features only relative to us. I have referred often to Heraclitus's perspectival mode. I therefore need to say that relativism is actually the opposite of aspect-seeing, of taking up different points of view on something, because the latter requires the assumption that there *is* something that stays put so that we may shift around it.

Heraclitus does, famously, say:

> The way up and the way down is one and the
> same. (60)

Again, the trite understanding, that this means that you climb up and down on the same trail, does not do him justice. Aristotle who has this Heraclitean way on his mind, takes it apart in his sober way: From here to there is *not* the same as from there to here, except that the distance is one; the meaning is different (*Physics* 202b19). But Heraclitus thinks exactly that: The meaning *is* one and the same. This following fragment is even more vulnerable to traipsy interpretation: Sea-water is both the cleanest and the foulest, since it is

> for fish drinkable and safe, but for men undrinkable
> and destructive. (61)

If this meant that certain items are good for some creatures and bad for others, it wouldn't be worth saying. I think, however, that both of these fragments intend something more original. The way and the water are *in themselves* both up *and* down, both safe *and* deleterious; the road goes up *by reason of* its opposing downness; the sea is safe *because of* its incorporated deleteriousness—but only when viewed from the aspect of a god, from a higher-level:

> To the god everything is beautiful and just, but men have understood some things as just, others as unjust. (102)

For what shows itself as ill to us is just what has given the good its potency, and the converse. The beauty that the god apprehends thus comes, it seems, from the cosmos's crisp order. It is a "both-and" order, undeterred in its factuality by the scruples of human talk-logic but not inaccessible to human thinking. For it is discernibly divided and discernibly collected by the communicating Logos. And this dividing and collecting is what the *philosophos*, the wisdom-loving man, repeats after the Logos (50). It is what Heraclitus does: "dividing according to nature" (1). As noted before, Socrates will later adopt Heraclitus's way as his own—the way of divisions *and* collections (*diaireseis* and *synagogeis*, *Phaedrus* 266b).

Recall here also that Heraclitus was the discoverer of transcendence, of the Wise Thing "separated" (*kechorismenon*) from everything (108); it is the word forms of which will later be used for distancing beings of thought from objects of sense (Aristotle, *Metaphysics* 1026a).

Indeed the later form is weaker, since where Heraclitus says "separated," Aristotle usually says only "separable" (*choriston*—its first sense, though often translated as "separate").

In conclusion, the picture of Heraclitus as the philosopher of ultimate instability, of radical mutability, is just ludicrous. Isn't the Logos at once the Design of a world-order, the Stuff in which it is realized, and its Speaker within the human soul? And isn't this governing Logos steadfastness in itself and the firm regulator of flux?

U. The Being of Parmenides

I now end the section on the Logos of Heraclitus with the Being of Parmenides. As I mentioned early on, the order of their coming on the philosophical scene is unsettled. As an issue of mere temporal precedence, who cares? But as a question concerning Heraclitus's motive-impulse—Was his thinking reactive or aboriginal?—one might be interested in determining the direction of influence of these two founders of Western philosophy.

This, however, seems to be impossible. We have no reason to think they ever met—given that they lived at opposite ends of the Greek world and that Heraclitus opted for immobility, while Parmenides apparently stopped his travels at Athens. I do think we might as well accept the tradition of people closer to him than we are. It makes Heraclitus the elder, claiming that he was born c. 540 and Parmenides c. 510 B.C.E. And in fact, the Heraclitean echoes some see in Parmenides' poem are very doubtful, certainly not dispositive.[31] To me it seems at least suggestive that the Stranger from Parmenides' Italian Elea who plays the chief role in Plato's *Sophist* commits "parricide" on his own Father Parmenides—meaning he refutes Parmenides' teaching that there is no Nonbeing and no negation and thus no logical opposition (241d).[32] Why would he need to do this philosophical murder, if Heraclitus had already done Parmenides in for him on this critical issue?

Since the attempt to decide on the basis of facts is futile, and the effort to determine actual influence is apt to fail, it seems best to me to suppose that both thinkers were self-moved in point of originality—referring not so much to their individual personalities as to their capacities to go to the origin and there to lay bare the roots of things. Hence the question of priority should be asked anew, in a different, speculative way: Is one of the two ways of thought inherently prior to the other? Is there a purely thought-based origin to philosophizing, one that is achronological?

I have been claiming that Heraclitus is not the philosopher of flux he was often represented to be, and that even the Eleatic Stranger's moderated summary of Heraclitus's philosophy—which states accurately his doctrine that "Being is many as well as one . . . For 'differing it is ever brought together,'" and ascribes it wittily to the more "tight-stretched (*syntonoterai*)" (242e) Ionian Muses (the Ionians, recall, were considered flabby in the West)—does not do justice to Heraclitus's discovery of cosmic unity and stability.

That corrected view of him would bring him closer to Parmenides, but it does not decrease the interest in their difference. For it is common experience that, as in matters of passion small differences can be most irritating, so in matters of thought the study of differences based on common intentions is most stimulating. If Heraclitus were simply a fluxist all the way down—as Parmenides does seem to be a monist and the philosopher of Being first and last—there would be no thought-provoking relation between them. Our tradition would just be radically dual at its origin, and we would be left with speculations about personal propensities. As it is, the two founders can be put—because they in fact *are*—into a time- and space-indifferent dialectic with each other. I might anticipate the outcome: The contest for intellectual priority is a draw, for its answer depends on our own urgencies. If we are longing for ontological grandeur and uncompromising plumbing of that one and only thought, Being, then Parmenides will seem the primordial deep thinker in his blazing induction into "the steadfast heart of persuasive truth" (Diels, Parmenides, 1, l. 29). But if we are gripped by the strife-locked unity of the physical cosmos and aroused by Heraclitus's unflinching heedfulness to that one Speaker, the Logos, then he will appear as the aboriginal penetrating observer in his solitary burrowing into the designs of the Wise Thing.

I might put it this way, incidentally justifying the large claim contained in the subtitle of this book, that Logos is the West's most *interesting* term: Being is surely our *deepest* term, since it betokens inexhaustible, perhaps inarticulable, plenitude. But Logos is surely our most interesting one, because it is articulation itself and carries huge but delimitable complexes of meaning. Being is largely mute substance, Logos mostly talkative relationality. (Serendipitously, the word "interesting" derives from Latin *inter-esse*, "to be among [things]" by way of relating to them: the prime power of the Logos is relation-making.) Better, however, to turn to texts.

From the—atemporal—Heraclitean perspective, Parmenides is the thinker of a Being un-rent by oppositions: The only way of seeking that thinking may employ is

> that [it] is and that [there] is no "is not." (Diels, Parmenides, 2, l. 3)[33]

The "it" comes from our English need for a pronoun. In Greek there is no "it," there is only "Is" (*esti*). It is a complete sentence: Saying, Thought, and Being all at once, conceived as the all-absorbent copula: *Issing* so to speak. It contains neither differences nor changes, it is

> one, continuous, for what descent will you seek for it? (8, l. 6)

The condition that seems to Parmenides

> whole, single-limbed, and also untrembling and complete (8, l. 4),

seems to Heraclitus untuned, relaxed—"everything gone by the board" (W 27). The greater point, though, is, that they both see the same, a Whole, an All, a One, and search out its nature. This is what makes them both First Philosophers in two senses: the earliest ones, and concerned with what Aristotle will call First Philosophy (*prote philosophia*) (*Metaphysics* 1026a): Its question, "What is Being?" is

> what is investigated of old, and also now, and ever and is ever perplexing. (1028b)

So I must say one last time: The notion that Heraclitus believed in ultimate universal flux, like a philosophical whirling dervish, is untenable. (An aside: Actually one shouldn't speak of thoughtful people as "believing in" things, and certainly not of Heraclitus and his brooding excogitations. He thinks, and he thinks he knows—as Aristotle disapprovingly noted.)

But notice must be taken of the fact that "Being" (*to on*) does not occur in our fragments of Heraclitus. His account of the being of the cosmos is not by way of Being but of Logos—a mindful collector, as well as a cosmic collection of opposing pluralities into a tensely connected unity.

Many distinctions fall out from the one between Being and Logos. At bottom, Parmenides has a one-sentence, indeed, one-word message:

> Only one story of the way
> Is left; that of Is. (8, l. 2)

This story is *his* first-person story, his poem; from him come the prescriptions and injunctions concerning proper speaking of Being. He assumes a near-priestly function as an initiate into the inner sanctum of Truth.

Heraclitus, on the other hand, utters medium-like what he hears from the Logos, and he expresses its Sayings in the terse style of an oracle. He speaks, to be sure, also from his own wide-ranging observation, psychic and physical (55), but his way is to direct attention away from himself personally: "Listen not to me but to the Logos" (50). Parmenides, on the other hand, takes his induction into the untrembling heart of truth very personally (1, l. 29)—a difference inviting speculation, though not for now.

Heraclitus, or rather the Logos, has a central truth as well:

One : Everything. (50)

It is characteristic that for Parmenides the copula, the expression of Being, swallows everything so that *it alone remains*, while for Heraclitus it disappears from between the terms so that *they alone show up*.

Thus:

Parmenides: Is. (8, l. 2)
Heraclitus: One Everything. (50)

Here is an antiphonal pattern based on the word *pan*, "all," that shows how close they are—and how far apart:

1. Parmenides: All (*pan*) is alike. (8, l. 22)
   Heraclitus: All things (*panta*) come to be by strife. (8)

2. Parmenides: All (*pan*) is together. (8, l. 5)
   Heraclitus: All things (*panta*) are one. (50)

3. Parmenides: All (*pan*) is continuous. (8, l. 25)
   Heraclitus: Out of all things (*panton*) one and out of one all things. (10)

Parmenides always says "All" in the singular, since his Being is undifferentiated, while Heraclitus says "All things" (or Everything), since his cosmos is a collection—but both say "All." The first couplet shows the difference between them: the All is united by homogeneity for the one, by discord for the other. The second couplet shows that both achieve unity, albeit by different routes. The third shows that where Being is first and last ever and only itself—"for Being draws nigh to Being"— the Logos works in self-opposing ways, now from the parts to the whole, now inversely. Can anyone deny that these two are about the same search, the search pursued of old and now and ever, even though the one—to return them to their proper order—thinks as a logologist (so to speak), the other as an ontologist? And that they set out for the future, for us, the two perennial, yet ever-evolving, terms of that inquiry: Logos and Being and its one paramount and never-resolved perplexity: One and/or Many?

IV

THE AFTERLIFE
OF THE LOGOS

Heraclitus's followers seem never to have settled into a proper school. "Such people don't become each other's students," Socrates says of them, "but they spring up on their own" (Plato, *Theaetetus* 180c). Probably he was too recalcitrant a guru, too much egregiousness incarnate, too wickedly distinctive, and too like a *daimon* become man to attract selfless loyalists. Thus the "Heraclitizers" and "Heracliteans" seem to have been a small sect. Perhaps some of them were a little nutty, tending to self-willed zealotry, to ludicrous apings of the master's outrageousnesses—the type a rebarbative guru would attract: "very high-toned" or "overwrought"; Plato's above-quoted adjective for their "Muses," *syntonoterai* (*Sophist* 242e), might bear these translations. The Heraclitean Logos, however, had a long and extensive afterlife: cycles of attributed misappropriations and unattributed appropriations. It was now adopted and adapted to perform a function in a new system, now selected for and subjected to an alien elevation in a new religion, now co-opted for curious polemical uses until finally—having entered common consciousness anonymously—its teaching emerged, I will claim below, as practical political wisdom.

Here are some high points of its later appearance. They are found in these authors, of whom I shall give very brief accounts.

Classical: Plato, Aristotle,
Old Stoa: Zeno, Chrysippos,
Christian: John the Evangelist,
Heretic-hunter: Hippolytus,
Neoplatonic: Plotinus,
Modern: Hegel, Schopenhauer, Nietzsche,

and, strange as it may seem,

American: Madison.

Plato (b. 427 B.C.E.) had, as I said, some connection to the Heracliteans, particularly to the above-mentioned Cratylus, whom he made the main character in the skeptical dialogue *Cratylus* (440c). But under the influence of Socrates, he had, as I imagine, divorced himself from them. In his *Theatetus* he lumps Heraclitus with the "wise men"—the Sophists, literally the crew of "wise-ists." He excepts only Parmenides, whom he evidently regarded as the much more serious predecessor. He relegates Heraclitus to the "all is born of flow and change" party (152e); he says that "the companions of Heraclitus are leading the chorus of this account (*logou*) very vigorously" (179d). But he makes no reference to *the* Logos; surprisingly, he ignores it; far from appropriating the Logos of Heraclitus, Plato eclipsed it.

And yet—the effect of Plato's early attachment to the Heracliteans seems to have been pervasive. Is not *the* Good both transcendent as even "beyond Being" and also immanent as active through everything in generating multiplicity, unifying it, and making it humanly intelligible (*Republic* 509b)? Are not the Platonic forms at once separable from the natural and human world and at work throughout these realms? Is not the great genus of the Other a way of coming to terms with opposition (*Sophist* 256e)? Are not human natures in opposition even through their virtues (*Statesman* 306b; see note 7 to this section)?

Aristotle (b. 384 B.C.E.) also undervalues Heraclitus, grouping him with the Physicists. As has been mentioned, this identification rests on the interpretation of Heraclitean fire as a "material cause" (*Metaphysics* 983b). Moreover he denigrates him, being quite out of sympathy with Heraclitus's intentional self-contradictions (1262a).

Old Stoa (c. 300 B.C.E.) is the periodizing name given to the first phase of antiquity's longest-lasting and most widespread philosophical movement, and the one of most consequence in modern times. These early Stoics are the true proto-moderns, especially in their representational theory of knowledge and their physicalism. For them Heraclitus's thoughts, transmutable into set doctrines, were found fodder. But they were as much his traducers as his inheritors, since they reinterpreted his terms to suit their technically sophisticated system. Here we find, on the one hand, these Heraclitean items: Fire as basic element, Zeus as Fire, Zeus as Logos and world-manager, the Logos as Fire.[1] On the other hand, their system is *meant* to be a genuine materialism with an underlying material *hyle* (an Aristotelian term) qualified as fire, and that is, I think, not true to Heraclitus. For his materialism turns out to be—like that of our scientists—as immaterial as any account, any *theory*, of matter, must needs be. In some cases the Stoics seem simply to have misread him: They took Heraclitus's flarings-up and dyings-down to imply a periodic total conflagration; but the Heraclitean transformations do not seem to be catastrophically discontinuous.[2]

The Stoics' chief elaboration is, indeed, built on a Heraclitean intimation. They understand the Logos-Fire to be *at once* an active and a passive principle. As "skillful fire" (*pyr technicon*) and also as Zeus-Logos, the world-manager, it is actively directive; as receptive material it is passively directed. Thus it is self-governed—and that is just what a Heraclitean equivocation suggests: the Wise Thing's maxim or design, which we should strive to know, is that by which "all things are steered" (passive voice) or "steer themselves" (self-active middle voice) through all things (41). The Stoics will fix this active-passive duality conceptually, all at once correcting and spoiling the ambivalent suspension in which Heraclitus had left it.

So all the Heraclitean terms turn up in the proper concatenations, but you couldn't recover the real Heraclitus from them; they are too system-bound. Heraclitus, like the Lord at Delphi, "neither hides nor tells but signifies" (93)—while the epigones formulate. It is the mode of latecomers.

John the Evangelist (1st century C.E.) is given here the merest, but unavoidable mention. His Gospel begins:

> In the beginning was the Word (*Logos*), and the
> Word was with God, and the Word was God.

A Logos that is speech and God at once would seem to be directly Heraclitean, but that is leaping to conclusions. John may have heard of God as Logos from the Stoics, or had in mind the biblical "Wisdom" of God (*hokhmah*, *sophia*, as in Proverbs 8:22 ff).[3] Indeed, Heraclitus and an earlier prophet do seem to sound the same tune: God is He

> Who hath measured the waters in the hollow of his
> hand, and meted out heaven with the span and com-
> prehended the dust of the earth in a measure, and

weighed the mountain in the scales, and the hills in a balance. (Isaiah 40:12)

But this is praise-singing, not a research project.

Hippolytus (3rd century C.E.) leads less far afield. He is one of the most copious sources of Heraclitean fragments and for the oddest reason. He serendipitously co-opted pagan Heraclitus for his own attack on the Christian heresy of one Noetus, who claimed that the Father *is* his own son and is thus simply identical with him. (Notice that in John's Gospel the identity is at first qualified: "was with.") Hippolytus got the idea of confuting Noetus by showing that his doctrine was really pagan because it was simply Heraclitean, specifically with respect to the coincidence of inverses (Father : Son :: Son : Father; see Section III E) and the divinity of the Logos.[4] For this purpose he quoted Heraclitus extensively (often in indirect discourse—"Heraclitus said that . . ."—and that accounts for the oblique syntax of some of the fragments). He does indeed get it right: Noetus seems to have been a Christian Heraclitus in a crucial respect—in identifying the world-transcending with the world-indwelling deity.

Plotinus (b. 205 C.E.) is chock full of Heraclitean allusions, though mellowed down. Here is the more diffuse, absorbable Heraclitus. (This sweeter version of Heraclitus's tart harmony goes back, as I have mentioned, to the Pythagorean *harmonia* composed of consonance-ratios, agreeable chords. In Plato's *Phaedo*

[95a], two Pythagorean-trained youngsters are right at home with an old tale in which Harmonia is presented as the daughter of Ares, god of war, and Aphrodite, goddess of love—the suave mythical melding of opposites.) Plotinus gives an almost lyrical description of the Logos-Fire, which is, for all that, recognizable as Heraclitean; it might have melted even Heraclitus himself:

> Fire itself is beautiful beyond the other bodies, because it has the rank-order of form in relation to the other elements. Above them in position, rarer than the other bodies as being incorporeal, it alone does not receive into itself the others, but the others receive it. ("On Beauty," *Ennead* 1.6, 3)

Nicholas of Cusa (b. 1401), mentioned above, is recalled here in passing both to shorten the leap into modernity and because his Coincidence of Opposites, reconciled in God, could be considered another case of Heraclitus being subjected to strife-mitigation.

In the early nineteenth century, with the burgeoning of historical research, collections of Heraclitus's fragments became available and incited a keen interest in the Early Greek philosophers, soon to be termed "Presocratics," a periodization that is, as I have thought, not always felicitous.

Hegel (b. 1770), as is ever his way with his predecessors, absorbs and assimilates Heraclitus dialectically, that is, as the human representative of the Idea's logical design realized in the world—as a thinker not fully self-aware, but dignified by his historical role as forerunner. A saying hesitantly attributed by Aristotle to Heraclitus in the *Metaphysics* (1005b) comes in handy for Hegel's purpose: "The same thing is and is not." It seems to me to be not really by Heraclitus, because he doesn't use bare ideal notions, and there occurs in the other fragments no hint of an analogue to the Hegelian triad Being, Nonbeing, and Becoming, the latter conceived as the dialectically achieved unity of the first two. Unlike Parmenides, Heraclitus does not employ "to be" existentially; when he does use a form of the verb, he always completes the predicate: to be this or that.

Hegel, however, contrives to credit Heraclitus with an albeit incompletely conceived prototype of Hegelian dialectic: "There is no proposition of Heraclitus that I did not accept in my logic," he says early in the Heraclitean chapter of *Lectures on the History of Philosophy*. So he puts Heraclitus, as I mentioned, after Parmenides, since Being is absolutely first in Hegel's dialectical development.

However, by virtue of taking Heraclitus completely seriously, Hegel comes on remarkable insights—the one author, as it seems to me, who does not bowdlerize him philosophically. He credits him with a true dialectic, a movement of thought, as he says, made into a principle: the Logos. In this Logos-dialectic, this thought-motion, Being (One) is the starting point and Becoming (Transformation) a second moment. Becoming, however, is indeed both generation and destruction, positive and negative at once, and so, in onto-logical terms it "is and is not." What Hegel slips into his account that is eminently un-Heraclitean is his own "sublation," the saving absorption of the antithetical phase into a new, positive culminating moment. Heraclitus, after all, *stops* at unresolved difference and preserves pervasive contradiction in thought and perennial antagonism in the cosmos: no conflict-resolution, no reconciliation.

Nonetheless, Hegel's recognition of Heraclitus as a particularly close fellow-dialectician seems to me, with qualifications, warranted. Hegel casts his logic, which is analogous to Heraclitus's *gnome*, the maxim, judgment, or design of the Wise Thing, into time. His predecessor does not speak of time but of change, and the change has repetitive cyclicality rather than culminating finality. Yet the Heraclitean Logos manifests itself in the world as does the Hegelian Spirit. Hegel has grasped the absence of explicitly named time in his predecessor, but he finds it—brilliantly—in a "concrete process." Fire, he says, "is physical time." That description seems to me to be an acute encapsulation: surely, if time *is* anything real, it is coming-to-be concretely regarded, though Heraclitus's "turns" of Fire are cyclical while Hegel's moments of dialectic are progressive. Heraclitean Fire is both always the same and always other, and both the cause of events and itself eventuation: it makes things happen and is itself the happening. I have been saying that Heraclitus has substituted ordered change for time. Hegel explains this: Fire is such designed change incarnate.

I think it is possible to place Heraclitus pretty precisely in Hegel's dialectical development—to pinpoint the dialectical moment he represents. It is "Force," which turns up in Hegel's *Phenomenology of Spirit* (A.3). This force is recognizably the same as the undefined notion on which Newton bases his dynamics. Hegel explicates it as a *relation*, a *substantial* relation, the very one I have tried to delineate above (Section III O–P).[5] Force expresses the substance of a thing insofar as *what it is depends on its relation* to other things and on their reciprocal relation to it. In a force-relation, a thing asserts its independence in an action whose effectiveness depends on the equal reaction of another thing: Nothing can be what it is unless it is locked into a relation of mutual assertiveness with another. Its inner being, its vitality, emanates as force seeking resistance. This is Heraclitean tension to a T. However, in the *Phenomenology*, force comes under Consciousness, the kind of knowing that has its object outside itself as an *other*. Self-consciousness, which recognizes *itself* in all its objects, stands higher in the dialectical development. Hegel would say Heraclitus is dialectically arrested. In the very beginning of his account of Heraclitus in the *History of Philosophy*, he credits him, to be sure, with taking a great step forward by understanding dialectic as a principle, objectively. I take this to mean that Heraclitus's dialectic is cosmic, that it is not a subjective way of thinking but the objective action of the Logos. As such it is an admirable beginning but a curtailed attempt, because it stops short of the completing synthesis, in which the object is reabsorbed into the subject.

As in the case of Parmenides the question, "Who was first in the nature of things?" was irresistible, so with Hegel is the question, "Who is last in the sense of having the final say?" And that seems to me to be Heraclitus, for an individually human as well as a world-historical reason. As far as the latter is concerned, I think the world's history shows no discernable upward-aiming logical finality such as Hegel's system sets out, but seems to be coming together and apart, as Heraclitus predicted, in tense stases and contentious transformations from now till doomsday. (And if there be a progression, it looks more like an expanding spiral whose rise through time is governed by one law: More.) As for the individual ultimacy, for having the last word on what philosophy is to be, I would claim it for Heraclitus, on the grounds that clearly discerning and exultantly entertaining cosmic contradictions and listening to a Logos that is other than himself brings him closer to the way things are than does systematic completeness. His very fragmentariness, a token of trying in the face of finitude, keeps philosophy alive past its scheduled expiration-date.

Schopenhauer (b. 1788) speaks, in *The World as Will and Representation*, of "cognitionless strife" as the blind force driving that unorganic nature which is the object of natural science (2nd book, para. 27). That drive is the first "objectivation" (that is, external expression) of the inchoate power of the primeval will, whose striving is to be finally annulled by the human renunciation of willing. This transmogrification of the vitally tensing Logos into a painfully compelling Power seems to me a crux of modernity and the stuff of a whole book.

Nietzsche (b. 1844) expresses what will be a lifelong veneration for Heraclitus in his early "Philosophy in the Tragic Era of the Greeks." He takes his co-opted predecessor to deny both the separation between thought and nature and the being of Being. He explains Heraclitus's paradoxes as the splendid result of the intuitive anti-rationalism that guides his representation of a force-replete world—as a sort of joyous, Whitmanesque "Do I contradict myself?/ Very well then I contradict myself, (I am large, I contain multitudes.)"[6] He sees him as what the Germans call a *Kraftmensch*, a reveler in his own overbearing strength and multifariousness.

However, Nietzsche's Heraclitus is, for all that, more peaceable than the real one: he understands becoming and passing-away "under the form of polarity" as the sundering of one power into two qualitatively, antithetically different activities *striving for reconciliation.*

In his late *Ecce Homo*, Nietzsche confesses that in Heraclitus's "general proximity his mood grows warmer than anywhere else," for he sees in him "the affirmation of passing away and destroying which is the decisive feeling of Dionysian philosophy" (3)—*this* of the despiser of drunk souls, the auditor of the designing Logos, the caster of a cold eye!

Nietzsche, I must think, is very likely the only human being to summon warm feelings toward this curmudgeonly solitary who discovered within his soul the science of nature, of a cyclically living cosmos, taut-braced by antitheses, disciplined by measure, bonded by ratio-related confronting terms, and governed both immanently and transcendently by Thinking itself—the Logos. Talk of willful misconstrual!

Madison (b. 1751), being an American, is out of order temporally and out of place geographically here; moreover I know no evidence that Heraclitus ever entered his reading or thinking. Yet I want to claim that this man, the most ingeniously practical of political philosophers, was a Heraclitean—proof that the ancient recluse knew not only the course of the natural world but also the way of the human world, knew it much as might a modern man.

Madison participated in the task of explaining and defending the Constitution he had had a chief hand in drafting, so as to secure its ratification. To this end he joined in the writing of a series of newspaper articles that became known as the *Federalist Papers*. One of the most famous of these, Number 10, addresses the causes and control of factions. A faction is a combination of people united by "some common impulse of passion, or of interest, adverse to the rights of other citizens . . . ," what we call an "interest group," especially of a fairly ruthless oppositional cast. "The latent causes of factions are sown into the natures of men." Hence they cannot be eradicated except by abolishing liberty, for liberty is to faction what air is to fire. To desire the annihilation of air, so essential to life, merely because it imparts to fire its destructive agency, asks for a remedy worse than the disease.

Thus for Madison faction and freedom, tension and vitality, are facts of humanity. Though the first purpose of government is to protect "the different and unequal faculties of acquiring property"—one might say, to maintain the natural ratio-relations—its second is to keep citizens from overstepping their proper measures. This control is exercised according to a wise design, the Constitution of a representative republic. Under it, factions, the expression of the ineradicable tensions of self-assertive human nature, take on the—unintended—role of mutual regulation; organized natural antagonisms produce a succession, now of tensed stases, now of vital shifts, that at once frustrate excess and invigorate self-expansion—like those wrestlers locked in a hold and looking for an advantageous reconfiguration. This Madisonian conception of 1781, which I do not think I have misrepresented by casting it in Heraclitean terms, is the political complement to the "invisible hand" of Adam Smith's economics.[7] Under its guidance people intent on competing, striving for their own gain, bring about a wealth-producing system of tensed balances and transformative crises. Thus a most fundamental aspect of American life is anticipated in the mordantly acute insights of a man, a philosopher, who stood aside from practical politics, yet announced a radical version of the Federalists' aim:

Greek: *ek panton hen* (10)

Latin: *e pluribus unum* (on the Great Seal and currency of the United States)

English: "out of many, one"

—not, however, by seeking what Europeans currently call "social harmony," but by asserting the mutual support of contesting energies.

A case can be made that the Founders' classical liberalism owes its success to the latitude it affords to the vigorous oppositionality of human nature. In other words: It honors the Heracliteanism of the world.

THE SOUL OF
HERACLITUS

Instead of translating Heraclitus's Logos I have circum-
and trans-scribed it. Let me now collect its features.

At the human level there is *logos*, the more or less
thoughtful utterance of our mind and its mindfulness
(*noos*, *phronesis*) (40, 2). At its best, it expresses not
the private thought of the speaker but rather listens to
and conveys the Saying of the Logos, the Wise; the style
of this expression, highly personal though it seems, is
in fact a reproduction of the sayings imparted by the
Logos. This Logos, which is divine but perhaps not a
nameable deity, governs and pilots the cosmos, the ordered world. It does so from within as a Wise Design,
a maxim or judgment that it does not have but *is*. By it
Everything, all the things that constitute the cosmos, are
unified, put into ordered relations: "Everything : One."
In its inner-worldly function, the Logos, as cosmic Fire,

ranges through the physical elements as their second nature, so to speak, as the fungible, measurable aspect of
their materiality, having the powers of elemental fire to
dissolve them, to break them down, as does an analyzing
intelligence. This Logos-Fire, then, at once instills and
discerns measures in the elements. By means of these
number-measures, the different elements are put into
fixed ratios with each other, which govern their transmutations into one another. Those constituents of the
cosmos that are directly opposed to each other, be it as
contraries or as contradictories, are also related, namely
in a taut bond of connecting tension. The Logos might
well be said to be ultimately responsible for all these
quantitative and qualitative ratios by which the cosmos
is held together in transformative or agonistic intimacy.
At any rate, the Greek name for ratios is *logoi*, and *logoi* are the cosmic unifying relations—call them the off-
spring, the utterances, the specifications of *the* Logos.
Moreover, immanently active though that thoughtful,
discerning Fire, that divinely ruling Logos of *logoi* may
be, it is also transcendent as the aforesaid Wise Design;
it is the Superlogos, *the* Logos, who not only manages
the cosmos from within but also informs it from beyond.

Having all these aspects in mind, I think the Logos
of Heraclitus needs no translation, but should simply
enter that most hospitable linguistic venue, English.
Our language is, after all, already loaded with somewhat mangled compounds of *logia*-endings, the -logy
terms from archaeology to zoology, and also of *legein*-
derivatives, of which "dialectic" is the philosophically

most potent. Transcription will allow logos to retain in English its whole burden of activities: collecting, counting, accounting, recounting, tale-telling; then ratio, relation, through to reason and all the derivative words for calculating, conversing, thinking—Language in all its internal origins and in its external manifestations, its utterance, that is, its "outering."

Recall that Heraclitus is told and hears of the Wise Design by which the Logos and its *logoi* both govern and pervade nature. Its message tells him that

Everything is wholly fated (By 63)

—which, the source of the fragment adds, is "the same as necessity."[1] Heraclitus means, I think, that nature is ruled by mathematico-physical compulsions imposed through ratio-relations. If Galileo will, famously, say that

the universe, which stands continually open to our gaze, cannot be understood unless one first learns to comprehend the language . . . in which it is written. It is written in the language of mathematics, and its characters are triangles, circles, and other geometric figures . . . ,[2]

then Heraclitus will have anticipated, even got ahead of him: Logos is *both* nature *and* its language, and it expresses itself in measures, that is, in numbers; in physics, the numbers of the calculating reason are more "modern" than the figures of the geometric imagination.

So, finally, how does Heraclitus himself come to know this language? By observing the apparent "tuning" (*harmonia*) of the cosmos and by grasping its unapparent "fitting" (also *harmonia*), its governing design. The former occurs primarily through the observant eye that sees the stringed lyre, the latter by the inner ear that hears the communicating Logos. What is the venue for this observant listening? It is the soul:

I have searched myself. (101)

While Parmenides rides a chariot right into the house of Being "which is outside of the path of men" (1, l. 27), Heraclitus walks the ways of his soul, which are boundless:

Setting out for the bounds of the soul, you would not find them out, though you passed along every way, so deep a Logos does it have. (45)

It is the original "depth-psychology": searching into oneself, exploring the never-ending ways of an enormously capacious inner place. Here, one last time, Heraclitus appears as a modern: Here is the subjective origin of the science of nature, that is, the mathematical construction of nature that proceeds from the human cognitive subject. This nature-construing soul is surely not a Freudian subconscious, an infernal place of imprisoned passion, for the description of which Freud borrows a line from Virgil:

> If I am unable to subdue Those Above, I will stir up
> the Place Below (*Acheronta*).[3]

It is instead a place of thought-pursuing passages, of
world-revealing ways. This is what I think: It is, in its
passable immensity, a *mirror* of the cosmos; to "search
myself" means to observe the soul-encompassed world
within as a reflection of the Logos- and *logoi*-informed
world without.

Recall, in support of this notion, Plato's *Timaeus*.
It presents a generative myth of the cosmos intended to
show why we can confidently make mathematical mod-
els of it. The reason is that it is itself copied from an ideal
model by a divine Craftsman. The world so designed is
exo-psychic—it has its soul wrapped around its body as
well as permeating it from within (36d–e). This world
soul is a concatenation of compounded ratios, so the
world is logos-enveloped and logos-imbued. It is, so to
speak, food for thought. Just so, Heraclitus had already
discovered the world within himself.

Moreover:

> The Logos of the soul is one that increases
> itself. (115)

So it must, for human thinking supervenes on observing
and listening, and therefore every observation expands
the human account—without making it the less *a logos*,
a collecting of multifariousness into unity. Thus, as the
man discovers more and more *logos*-relations, passes
over more ways, the Logos grows in comprehensiveness.

It is a familiar effect of habitual introspection: more self-knowledge produces more self to know, and as the explored soul expands, so does the knowledge of the divine Logos itself and of the cosmos it rules and inhabits. (There *is* a faint premonition here of the Hegelian System. Hegel's dialectic too recovers Nature's realization of God's Logic as a science of Mind, for Nature is externalized Spirit [Section IV].)

Is this capacity of soul Heraclitus's alone? Is his activity eccentric, "outside the paths of men?" Not at all:

It is possible for *all men* (my italics) to know themselves and to be soundminded (*sophronein*). (116)

This saying is just what the two inscriptions on the portal sides of the Temple of Apollo at Delphi will famously enjoin, "Know thyself" and "Nothing too much"—the proverbial formulas for self-comprehension and moderation (the usual translation of *sophrosyne*, whose literal meaning is "soundmindedness"). But Heraclitus can't have gotten his own human wisdom from the not yet existent temple,[4] any more than Socrates, his successor in exhorting humans to practice sane inwardness, needed those priestly saws, famous as Greek wisdom—and, infamously, not Greek practice. What is, I think, most to be remarked in this fragment is its human universality. Heraclitus is a curmudgeon but not a misanthrope. His against-ness is tough for-ness.

Socrates will, nonetheless, cite the first Delphic maxims as guiding his own activity. He will, he says, eschew sophisticated construals of worldly myths in favor of knowing his own inner constitution (*Phaedrus* 229e, also *Protagoras* 343b). But Socrates had given up on the "inquiry into nature" early on, precisely because the Physicists made no use of a piloting principle (*Phaedo* 96); Heraclitus has the greater faith both in the physics-capabilities of the psyche and in the corresponding rationality of the physical world.

I think Heraclitus is first, or if not first—for who can ever prove primacy in thought?—at least all on his own, in going within; indeed, derivativeness in this matter would be self-contravening. Moreover, he knows just why this introspection is not an invitation to that inward idiosyncrasy (literally, "private temperament") for which we have the euphemism "subjectivity." The reason is that there is a two-fold commonality to our thinking: It is both a common capacity of humankind, and it is concerned with what is in its very nature common. Thus:

> Common (*xynon*) to everyone is thinking (*to phronein*). (113)

Heraclitus once more puns on *xynon* and *xyn nooi*, "common" and "with mind." And also:

> Those who [wish to] speak with mind (*xyn nooi*) must make themselves strong in the Common (*toi xynoi*) to all, just as a city [should] in its law—and much more strongly. For all human laws are nour-

ished by the One, the Divine. For it rules as largely as it wants and is sufficient to everything and is [so even] over and above. (114)

Note that the Divine, surely the Logos, rules within the political community as the source of law, and also beyond as the cause of cosmic unity. And since "the Common" has just been, by means of punning homonymy, identified with mind itself, the Logos rules in the cosmos, in the city, in the mind—everywhere and for everyone.

Yet in spite of the universality of the encounter and the common capacity, humankind does not listen often. Men will not do what they could do:

It is necessary to follow the Common. For although the Logos is common (or "with mind"), the many live as having private thought. (2)

Again, the pun: Logos is both "common" and "with mind," that is to say: there for all men and matching the human mind. Perhaps these disparaging reflections on man's recalcitrant particularism brought it about that Heraclitus became known, in contrast to the "Laughing Philosopher" Democritus, as the "Weeping Philosopher,"[5] though he seems more irritated than weepy. In any case, it would be, I think, a misconstrual to regard him as sad and sorry over the strife-imbued world. Resolution is, after all, dissolution, so he finds antagonisms bracing, even wonderful; it is human incorrigibility that gets up his ire—but maybe that's invigorating too.

The most private, most mindless state is dreaming—no revelations from the repressed unconscious here; thus also no responsibility:

> For those who are awake there is a single and common cosmos; each of those who are asleep turns himself away to the private one. (89)

The contrasting pair "common cosmos : private world" is at the center of Heraclitus's psychology—or rather of his cosmo-psychology. It does not, I think, betoken what we moderns would first think of—oppositions such as "public : private" or "political : personal" or "social : individual." It goes beyond these various community-bound antitheses. Yet neither, clearly, does the pair oppose the cosmopolitanism of the *polis*-leaver, the world-wanderer, to the parochial stay-at-home. Just as Socrates never thought to leave an unsympathetic Athens (except for military service, *Crito* 52), so Heraclitus did not need to leave uncongenial Ephesus whose despised citizens had "private minds," at least not for another city.[6]—The Common was not to be searched for among the terrestrial varieties of humanity. The Logos-listener, the soul-searcher, finds that the Logos-steered Cosmos is the true Common and that Logos-deafness and dreaming world-aversion are the real privacy and privation.

There may even be—and now I'm speculating—a hint of hoped-for human community in Heraclitus's turn to the Common, something like the idea expressed in a proverb Phaedrus offers Socrates in the dialogue named for him. As they part, Phaedrus quotes: "Friends have things in common (*koina ta ton philon*)" (276c). This is usually understood as a proverb saying that friends share their wealth, but it could also be heard to mean "The Common Things are what [properly] belong to friends," as if what is in its very nature common, cosmically common, is what brings us humanly together and rescues us from stultifying privacy. For Heraclitus, it is the Logos, the Wise, that is the Common; for Socrates, it is the Thinkable, the *noeton*, the *idea*. For both, the communion of friendship was, I am imagining, grounded in these commonalities. Heraclitus, however, seems to have found that such friends were not tolerated in Ephesus (121).

Why is it possible for the human soul to be at once part of, and yet self-excluded from, the world-order? Souls are exhaled from, vaporized out of, moisture (*ton hygron anathymiontai*) (12). Presumably, intelligent fire has a part in this conversion of the wet element:

The flash-dried [or dry] soul is wisest and best (118),

while the stumbling drunk has a sodden soul (117). Evidently this wetting of the soul is a sort of living regression to its birth-element, to its pre-birth condition before its fiery sublimation, but also to its post-mortem dissolution:

For souls it is death to become water, and for water to become earth; and from earth comes water, and from water soul. (36)

Here the soul is placed within its cycle of transformations—through water, earth, water, back to soul by exhalation. This wet origin and end stays with the soul and appears in its pleasures:

> It is a delight—or death—for souls to become
> wet. (77)

So the soul takes part in the universal elemental transformations of the cosmos, and that explains why it is capable of obtuseness: It may be deleteriously, wetly, immattered. Hence it is not a trans-material substance—and yet, it also *is*, for in a behind-the-scenes sense, when most truly soul, it is ever fiery, dried to incandescence by the agency of thoughtful Fire. But then again, the same holds of all the inanimate cosmic elements. So does the soul, or does it not, differ from sensible bodies? In *On the Soul*, where he gives a thumbnail history of his own predecessors, Aristotle interprets thus:

> Heraclitus also says that the ruling principle (*arche*)
> is soul, since [it is] the exhalation (*anathymiasin*),
> from which he constitutes the other things. And
> indeed it is the most incorporeal and ever-flowing,
> and he, as many others, thought that what is moved
> is known by what is moved, and that the things that
> are, are in motion. (405a)

Is there an answer here? Is not even a "most incorporeal," a very volatile, exhalation a body? But perhaps the whole passage is misleading; note that in Fragments 12 and 36 above, the soul itself is an exhalation of moisture, thus not a first source.

I have argued that the Heraclitean flux-theory is a misconstrual. I think, therefore, that the notion of the fluid soul as the principle of everything is an effect of Aristotle's retrofitting Heraclitus into his own preoccupation with the principle of movement in nature, for surely Heraclitus's dry soul is an immense territory and nothing like a flux. Nor is there anything in our fragments that suggests that the soul is constitutive of the external cosmos, except insofar as it takes part in the cosmic cycle. And yet it is not unlike the cosmic Fire, which is both a particular bodily element and a pervasive intelligence, and thus does seem to be closely akin to the human soul. It structures a nature that regards, signals, addresses us:

> *La nature est un temple où des vivants piliers*
> *Laissent parfois sortir de confuses paroles;*
> *L'homme y passe à travers des forêts de symboles*
> *Qui l'observent avec des regards familiers.*

> Nature is a temple whose living pillars
> Sometimes allow confused words to emerge;
> Man passes there through forests of symbols
> Which observe him with familiar looks.
>   (Charles Baudelaire, "Correspondances")

So I imagine that the soul is in one aspect a pervasive, transformable matter and in another a particular, personal intelligence; it is envelopingly cosmic and individually human.

This human soul, Heraclitus's soul, is possessed of a specifically human way of being in the world: It is an early, maybe a first, instance of what will come to be called "intentionality," the remarkable capacity, peculiar to thinking, of "aboutness," of containing its object within itself, such that it is at once *before* the mind and *of* the mind. That is, I imagine, how Heraclitus's own soul both held and beheld the cosmos, which spoke to it oracularly.

My near-last fragment, as famous as the flux fragments, is usually rendered as "A man's character is his destiny." It sounds pleasantly portentous, and we've heard it often, but what does it mean? Does it say that we are responsible for our fate or the opposite? Does it claim that the moral stamp on our nature frees us to shape our life or that it consigns us to follow its necessities? It seems a different translation is needed. Here is the fragment again, practically in transcription:

Ēthos is *daimon* to a man. (119)

Daimon is here, I think, not destiny but "divinity," as in this fragment:

A man is called "infant" in relation to (*pros*) a divinity (*daimon*) as is a child in relation to man. (79—one last case of a continuous proportion)[7]

And *ēthos* in Fragment 119 is not "individual character" but our sort, our "kind"—humankind, as in this fragment:

> Human-kind (*ēthos anthropon*) does not have
> insight (*gnome*); the divine-kind (*theion*) has it. (78)

Then the fragment in question might go:

> His kind is man's divinity,

meaning:

> Humanity is man's divinity,

a very Heraclitean paradox. Although from one perspective, "the wisest of men appears as a monkey in wisdom and beauty and everything compared to the god" (83), I cannot imagine that a man whose soul held and heard the same cosmos within that his eyes saw and observed without, thought of himself much as a monkey. Indeed, from another aspect, human beings have the life of divinity within them:

> Immortals : mortals : : mortals : immortals—
> [mortals] living the death of those [immortals]
> and [immortals] having died the life of those
> [mortals] (62)[8]

—a last citation of the identificatory chiasmus (Section III E, M).

The chiasmus, recall, unifies inverses. Gods, the fragment announces, are related to men inversely as men to gods. Thus they are locked into each other; they are more than oppositionally paired. They are reciprocally dependent, antithetically identical.

For men "live the death" of gods. I think this means that their living deathboundness, their mortality, is the condition for the immortality of the gods; *im*-mortals (*a-thanatoi*) are, after all, mortals (*thnetoi*) of negative quality. Men live the gods' death *for* them.

Reciprocally, the gods *have died* the life of men. They are in the completed state of death, beyond the dying done by mortals. But *being* thus past dying, they live, as dead, the life available for living mortals—perhaps not for all, but for the listeners to the deep Logos in the soul.

This thought had staying power. On his last day Socrates will say that those who during their lives "take hold of philosophy rightly study nothing but dying and being dead" (*Phaedo* 64a). He means that within mortal life they escape to post-mortem eternity.

Heraclitus, too, has a high regard for mortals who live, within this life, the death of the immortals, for humans who, though yet living, reach the afterlife where living and dying have ended. These

> philosophical men must inquire into many
> things, (35)

for they must learn how "everything is one."

Such *philosophoi*—it is one of the earliest appearances of the word, and Heraclitus still uses it adjectivally—have specific human excellences, as in this, the last fragment I shall cite:

> To be soundminded: the greatest excellence (*arete*).
> And wisdom: to say true things and to *do* [them],
> giving heed in accordance with nature. (112)

And one last time, translators differ: ". . . to say what is true and to act giving heed to the nature of things," or, as seems right to me, ". . . to say true things and *do* them . . ."[9] For Heraclitus's verb *poiein* doesn't really bear the usually intransitive sense of "to act," but rather means "to do or execute" something.

* * *

Here starts a new chapter: What does it mean to *do* true things? The Logos of Heraclitus obligates us to *speak* in agreement with itself (50); how does it want us, as humans in our humanity, to *do* its truth? There are fragments to answer this question that I won't consider here, for this little book was about the Logos of Heraclitus, his divinity. Another, yet smaller, might be about his Ēthos, his humanity. Probably that ēthos will follow in the way of the Logos, for recall that the Logos itself *does* what it says (Section III N–O). It speaks to us, saying One : Everything, and that is its doing as well.

So let me return for a summation to that Logos and the Soul in which it manifests itself. I imagine that Heraclitus first heard his, or rather *the* Logos within, delivering its sayings in the language of his mind. In pursuing its call through the pathways of his boundless soul, he found a psychic cosmos congruent with the physical one present to his observant eye. Thus, looking without and listening within, he came on the Wise Design that keeps everything antagonistically together and learned to articulate, in pungently precise Greek, his—and everyone's—Logos.

POSTSCRIPT

By a reasonable reckoning, Heraclitus was writing down the sayings imparted to him by the Logos roundabout 490 B.C.E.[1] The above appreciation was completed in 2010 C.E., almost exactly two-and-a-half millennia (or, by one ancient convention, one hundred generations) afterwards. To me it seems wonderful that these sayings have not lost their engaging immediacy—wonderful in itself and as a testimony to the insignificance of temporal passage in the presence of thinking.

NOTES

I. The Figure of Heraclitus

1. John Pope-Hennessey, *Raphael: The Wrightsman Lectures* (New York: NYU Press, 1970). Detail of Heraclitus, pl. 91. This figure was added later to the original fresco of 1510.

Like all that follows in this essay, the identifications of the figures, including that of Heraclitus, are speculative and subject to challenge. Nor are the titles of the frescos Raphael's own. Moreover, there is a dispute about the so-called "*Disputa.*" It may depict an exaltation of the Eucharist rather than a controversy about it. I notice, however, that at least one of the identified saints on each side of the picture was known to have taken sides in the argument. Gregory, on the left, defended the "real presence" of Christ's body in the Host, whereas Augustine, on the right, was known as a "symbolist."

The terms of this debate, I want to point out, are felicitously germane to a, perhaps *the*, Heraclitean issue: Is his Logos real, material, or a representation in human terms of divine wisdom (see Section III R, "Sensible Paradoxes")? For the adaptation of Heraclitean terms to Christian contexts, see Section IV.

2. Diogenes Laertius 9.5 (3rd cent. B.C.E.). He wrote a compendium of the lives and opinions of philosophers which contains many quotations. Heraclitus's Milesian predecessors, the "Physicists," if they wrote books at all, seem to have written prose, so Heraclitus is the first writer of philosophic prose only insofar as he is acknowledged as the first philosopher.

Concise locutions are the vital spirits alike of poetic and aphoristic speech; wordiness makes prose prosaic. Here is an example:

> Heraclitus: "Multi-learnedness does not teach [one] to have insight." (40)

> Schopenhauer: "[A] man may have a great mass of knowledge, but if he has not worked it up by thinking it over for himself it has much less value than a far smaller amount which he has thoroughly pondered." ("On Thinking for One's Self")

3. The order seemed settled in favor of Heraclitus for a while, but the issue has been reopened (Section III U).

4. The broad significance I will claim for Heraclitus's *logos* below is controversial (see Robinson, pp. 75, 114). In this brief account I can't give all the counter-arguments the notice they deserve.

5. Aristotle (*Metaphysics* 987a) speaks of Plato and Socrates as coming "after" the people who are now denominated as coming "before" Socrates; that is, as being pre-Socratic. It seems to have been Friedrich Schleiermacher who, in an address "Über den Werth des Socrates als Philosophen" (1815), established the periodizing notion that Socrates' thought was pivotal in philosophy. Before him, Schleiermacher argues, different groups of philosophers pursued different kinds of philosophy, after him the kinds were still discriminated, but every school cultivated all kinds.

Insofar as "Presocratic" could be taken as "not quite up to Socrates," it might be good to forget the term. Though he depicts their admiration as mutual, Plato in fact, and very convincingly, shows old Parmenides as able to run dialectical circles around young Socrates (*Parmenides* 131 ff). And Heraclitus, to whose party Plato belonged in his youth, would have scintillated in conversation with him—I don't know about mutual admiration.

The anecdote of the Delian diver is told by Diogenes Laertius 2.22.

6. Almost all the fragments are cited here by their plain numbers (enclosed in parentheses) in the major edition: *Die Fragmente der Vorsokratiker*, trans. Hermann Diels, ed. Walter Kranz, vol. 1, 1903. Later editions were revised or reprinted. (Berlin: Weidmannsche Verlagsbuchandlung, 1954. I used this printing). The fragments are often cited as D or D-K, plus the Diels number. Even editions other than Diels's in which the fragments are renumbered to express the editors' own interpretation, refer to this numbering either in the text or in a concordance.

The D-numbering itself is the fruit of a wise counsel of despair; it is simply alphabetical according to the source-author's name (1.viii). Thus the Diels order is rationally irrational in making no sense but in avoiding premature commitment to any speculation.

Some fragments rejected by Diels are cited here by a "By" or "W" number: I. Bywater, *Heraclitus of Ephesus*; Philip Wheelwright, *Heraclitus*.

A word on the term "fragment," which is used by Diels, and by writers before and after, of all the Presocratic *reliquiae*, "remains" or "remnants." It does not mean that the sentences are all fragmentary, but pertains to the fact that no complete work has survived. Oddly enough, one reason may have been—as I imagine—that late-comers quoted these precursors so often that no one missed the complete texts.

Except where otherwise noted, all the translations are mine, of course with the help of predecessors.

II. The Word *logos*

1. Aristotle, *Physics* 186b.

2. In German, too, there is counting, *zählen*, and recounting, *erzählen*.

Attention to the collecting function of *logos* seems to me the most suggestive contribution of Martin Heidegger's essay "Logos (Heraclitus Fragment 50)" and also of a colloquium: Martin Heidegger and Eugen Fink, *Heraclitus Seminar, 1966/67.* The protagonists did a lot of heavy heaving with no determinate outcome I can express to myself; it was a mandarin-like contest between a great man and his independently intelligent disciple.

The general meanings of *logos* come to me mostly from Liddell and Scott's *Greek-English Lexicon* and H. Frisk's *Griechisches etymologisches Wörterbuch.*

III. The Logos of Heraclitus

1. See Diels, p. 161, note on l. 17.

2. The most notorious case is the Oracle's reply to Croesus, King of Lydia. He inquired whether he should go to war with Cyrus, King of Persia. He was told that if he went he would destroy a great empire. He did go and did destroy an empire—his own (Herodotus, *Persian Wars* 1.53, 91).

3. Diogenes Laertius says that Heraclitus finally went misanthropic and took to the mountains. He recites a slew of insults he administered to his Ephesians. But this fragment alone is testimony enough:

> The Ephesians, all of them who are of age, deserve to
> hang themselves and leave the city to the youngsters.
> (121, also 125a)

4. These reports are, to be sure, unreliable. Diogenes Laertius, who notes Heraclitus's remark (9.5), also reports that one Sotion said Heraclitus attended Xeophanes's lectures. The Pythagorean was Hippasus (Wheelwright, p. 114, n. 7).

5. Diogenes Laertius says that the compositions mentioned in Fragment By 17 above were Pythagoras's own, though early Pythagorean tradition was evidently entirely oral (Diels, p. 96).

For Pythagorean mathematics and the appropriation of the word *logos* for the ratio-relation, see Guthrie, *Pythagorean Sourcebook*, p. 24 ff. and passim; see also Kirk and Raven, chap. 7.

For Pythagoras's introduction of the term "philosophy," see Diels, p. 544, l. 35; for "cosmos" see Diels, p. 105, l. 24.

For the post-Heraclitean date of Pythagorean number-ontology, see Kirk and Raven, p. 236 ff. Aristotle says that for them "number was the beingness (*ousia*) of all things (*panton*)" (*Metaphysics* 987a).

6. I must mention here the monographs by Jüngl and Kurtz that are probably now quite inaccessible but were very helpful. The latter contains a welcome review of scholarship on Heraclitus's Logos going back to Schleiermacher (1808).

7. Florian Cajori, *A History of Mathematical Notation*, vol. 2 (Chicago: Open Court, 1929), p. 189. For the introduction of the colon to symbolize division by Leibniz, see ibid., vol. 1, p. 271.

8. Not until the seventeenth century; see Jacob Klein, *Greek Mathematical Thought and the Origin of Algebra* (1934), trans. Eva Brann (New York: Dover Publications, 1992), p.211 ff.

9. *The Thirteen Books of Euclid's Elements* (2nd ed., 1925), vol. 2, trans. with commentary by Sir Thomas Heath (New York: Dover, 1956). Book 5 contains the general theory of proportion, which includes incommensurable magnitudes, p. 112 ff. Book 7 contains the special theory of proportion for numbers, p. 177 ff. The relevant definitions with Heath's commentary introduce Book 5.

10. Greek mathematicians were in possession of an extensive inventory of geometric lines incommensurable with each other, and approximations of their number ratios were worked out. But these were never accepted as true, finitely articulable numbers, the kind expressible symbolically by radicals, such as the length of the diagonal of a square with side 1. Moreover, the possibility that the essential characteristic of a geometric line, its continuity, might be in a one-to-one relation to a new number type, the irrational or "real" (!) numbers, was not formally shown until 1872, by Dedekind in his "Continuity and Irrational Numbers." He spoke of them as a "creation."

11. First by Al Khoraswarizmi (9th century). D. E. Smith, *History of Mathematics*, vol. 2 (New York: Dover Publications, 1953), p. 252.

12. Fire is also precisely the missing element in the surviving fragments of Heraclitus's putative teacher, Xenophanes of Colophon. In his cosmogony, earth was the basic element out of which and into which everything is transformed. He mentions the air above, the boundless below, and water, each presumably transformable (Diels, Xenophanes, 27–29). Too little of his writings survives for him to figure prominently among the "Physicists."

13. The following references are to Kirk and Raven. Thales: "most causative," p. 90, no. 89; Anaximander: "what is owed," p. 117, no. 112; Anaximenes: "rarity and density," p. 144, no. 143.

I might say here that fire in some form appears in all the predecessors, but not as basic.

14. Not that Aristotelian self-movement is quite intelligible, for it requires the self-splitting of the moving principle within a nature; the best example of that which has a nature is an animal, and a whole animal moves itself because "there is distinguished that which moves and that which is moved" (*Physics* 254b).

15. Without article (*sophon*) 50, 108; with (*to sophon*): 32, 41. I have a sense that Heraclitus puts plain *sophon* in mental quotation marks.

16. The only other major philosopher (whom I know of) to think in this mode is Spinoza.

17. The notion of a tone-dynamics, a tension between tones that makes melody come alive, is taken from Victor Zuckerkandl, *Sound and Symbol: Music and the External World*, Bollingen Series 14 (Princeton: Princeton Univ. Press, 1973), p. 20.

I should say here that the Pythagoreans, if not Pythagoras himself, had a cosmology based on the musical *harmonia*, an arithmological astronomy that included the "music of the spheres" (Guthrie, *Pythagorean Sourcebook*, pp. 28 and 50, n. 20). Heraclitus's cosmology has a feature not present to Pythagorean mathematics: force (Section III Q).

18. No one else translates this fragment as I do, but I stick to the actual Greek. This fragment is difficult to construe as it has come down to us.

19. Ida Freund, *The Study of Chemical Composition: An Account of Its Method and Historical Development* (1904) (New

York: Dover Publications, 1968), p. 143. This is the classic account of an era when the law had been empirically investigated for many substances over a century (chap. 5). It is the first law listed in my old chemistry textbook.

The Heraclitean enterprise described below is carried on in Plato's *Timaeus*, but on very different principles (49 ff.). There elements are not transformed into each other but reconfigured through their underlying geometric constitution and not by the measure-imparting agency of a hyper-element such as Heraclitus's Fire. Some numerical ratios are indeed given by Plato, but they are combination- not transformation-relations. Thus, whereas for Heraclitus 2 units of water transform under Fire into 1 unit of earth (i.e., water:earth::2:1, whether by weight or volume is uncertain), in the *Timaeus*, physical, sensible elements must be reduced, for example by ordinary fire, to the geometric traces, namely plane triangles, from which the ideal solids underlying the physical elements were constructed. These traces can recombine into new elements. Thus the trace geometry of 1 unit of water recombines into 2 of fire and 1 of air (i.e., fire:air::2:1, when the trace triangles of water combine anew). Moreover, physical elements as such "never go into another form." They are untransformable (*Timaeus* 56d–e). This is a differently conceived chemistry from that of Heraclitus; it is a more ultimately mathematical theory.

Here is a task worth attempting: to consider whose account can be rightly called more modern.

20. See Julian Barbour, *The End of Time: The Next Revolution in Physics* (Oxford: Oxford Univ. Press, 2000).

21. Hippolytus, in bk. 9 of *The Refutation of All Heresies*, as quoted by Wheelwright, Fr. 30, p. 141; also Kirk, p. 352.

22. Logos is called "common and divine," by Sextus Empiricus 8.132, quoted in Wheelwright, pp. 21, 119, n. 4. "War and Zeus are the same thing," is from Philodemus, quoted in Wheelwright, p. 120, n. 3.

23. A fine example of confronting the Logos with logic is Jonathan Barnes's *The Presocratic Philosophers: The Arguments of the Philosophers*. One method is to fix what Heraclitus meant, usually in latter-day categories, and next to formalize

that extracted meaning. It then turns out that "by our standards" Heraclitus produced paralogisms. I have every faith in the formalizations and deep doubts about the extracted meaning. The outcome is that Heraclitus seems to be driven into either logical fallacy or philosophical weirdness.

24. This might be the place to distinguish nonverbal and verbal ratios from irrational ones. The nonverbal, or nonverbalizable, ratio-relations would be just those between the sensuous experiences of events or things that Heraclitus needed Fire to bring into a proportion, one of whose ratios expressed measures (Section III N). The purely verbal ratios are the terms of metaphor as understood in this section, figures of *speech*. Simile, incidentally, differs from metaphor in making the similarity or likeness—or unlikeness—on which both depend explicit: "My mistress' eyes are nothing like the sun" (Shakespeare, Sonnet 16). Thus simile can be mordant because it is bald—the lesser trope.

The irrational ratios were a scandal for the Pythagoreans, who discovered them. They came on certain lines seated in geometric figures, such as the side and diagonal of a square, that were provably incommensurable with each other, that is, had no common unit of measure, and therefore had no ratio expressible in acceptable numbers. (We say that side : diagonal :: 1 : $\sqrt{2}$. But the symbol $\sqrt{2}$, which stands for the whole endless non-repeating decimal that fails to express the irrational number, was not devised until the later seventeenth century.) The shock to Pythagoreans consisted in the fact that incommensurables threw into doubt their number-ontology, which asserted that the world was basically constituted of natural numbers, especially of the first ten.

Book 5 of Euclid's *Elements* set out, as was said above, the theory of ratios of incommensurables (of which commensurable magnitudes are a subclass).

25. This return to mere numerosity in physics is actually a—not always conscious—reapproaching to the number-ontology of the Pythagoreans. Tradition-conscious physicists acknowledge them as their avatars, as does, for instance, Feynman (Richard P. Feynman, Robert B. Leighton, and Matthew Sands, *The Feyn-*

man Lectures on Physics [Reading, Mass.: Addison-Wesley Publishing Company, 1963], vol. 1, pp. 50–51).

26. Rogers, pp. 129–30, n. 27. The diagram in the note shows a) the tensile force *at the tips*, b) the resultant force of 0 *within the string*, c) the irrelevance to the tips' bending *of the stretching* of the string.

27. Carved c. 610 B.C.E., Pentelic marble. National Museum, Athens, No. 3476. The base is Attic (Mount Pentelicus was the source of marble for Athenian sculpture), and so it surely was never seen by Heraclitus, who declined to travel—except within himself (Section V). Diogenes Laertius says that he was invited by King Darius to the Persian court and brusquely declined. Moreover, he despised the Athenians, although they admired him, and preferred to stay at home with his Ephesians, who returned his scorn of them (9.15). All this could well be made up, except for his sedentary ways, which ring true.

28. Aristotle usually treats his predecessors' logical slackness with no-nonsense severity, but in the interests of a higher sense, he is not himself immune from suggestive self-contradiction. For what else but a contradiction in terms is his wonderful definition of motion as "incomplete"—*not* incomplet*ed* but terminally incomplete—"fulfillment" *energeia . . . ateles* (*Physics* 201b)? It doesn't help that he qualifies it as "a sort of *energeia*."

29. Once again "Common" is without an article, but so are all the true nouns.

30. They are included neither by Bywater nor Diels.

31. The main trace of Heraclitus said to occur in Parmenides' poem (Diels 6, l. 7) is where he speaks of "a back-turned (*palintropos*) path." He is referring to the way of those who think that "to be and not to be are the same." However, there is no such "path" (*keleuthos*) in the Heraclitean fragments, but a "way" (*hodos*) that is "up and down" (60). Nor is there *palintropos*, if I am justified in reading "back-stretched" (*palintonos*) in the bow-and-lyre fragment (51), where the word appears modifying *harmonia*, and some would read *palintropos*. But what could a "back-*turned* harmony" mean?

As for the argument in favor of Parmenides' priority, its main twentieth century proponent was Karl Reinhardt (1916). Most recently, the debate has been revived by Catherine Osborne in "Heraclitus," pp. 38, 95–96.

Hegel had already put Parmenides before Heraclitus in his *History of Philosophy* (1816), as one would expect of him: in his dialectical order Being comes before Nonbeing and Becoming (Section IV).

32. As Heraclitus did not need an explicit Law of Contradiction to contravene it intentionally, so Parmenides could not have invented it, as is sometimes claimed. For he thinks not that it is *false* to assert Being and Nonbeing at once but that it is *impossible*, since any negation is unthinkable: "It can neither be uttered nor thought that *not is*, *is*" (8, ll. 8–9). Who proscribes the impossible?

33. Most translations of this line run something like: ". . . that it is and cannot be." "Is" and "can[not] be" or "is [not] possible" render the same verb *esti*, which, when accented, does mean "is possible." (Accents were not invented until c. 200 B.C.E.) I don't think Parmenides meant, in the first instance, that Nonbeing *is not possible* but that it *is* not. If it were thought to be impossible it would be conceivable, but that is just what he denies.

IV. The Afterlife of the Logos

1. Stoic sources: *Stoicorum Veterum Fragmenta*, vols. 1–4, ed. Hans von Arnim (1902–25) (reprinted, New York: Irvington Publishers, 1986). Examples in order of mention: In vol. 1, p. 27, l. 12; p. 42, l. 9. In vol. 2, p. 139, l. 40; p. 315, l. 3; p. 116, l. 13.

The conflagration: F. H. Sandbach, *The Stoics*, 2nd ed. (Indianapolis: Hackett Publishing, 1994), p. 79.

Stoics and modernity: Eva Brann, *Feeling Our Feelings: What Philosophers Think and People Know* (Philadelphia: Paul Dry Books, 2008), chap. 4.8.

2. The main passage, attributed to Heraclitus by Plutarch but now generally rejected, refers to such a conflagration, see Wheelwright, p. 124, n. 22.

3. C. K. Barrett, *The Gospel According to St. John: An Intro-duction with Commentary and Notes on the Greek Text* (London: S.P.C.K, 1965), p. 128.

4. For Noetus's heresy, see Kirk, p. 65. His total identification of God and the Word, that is, God and Christ the Son, is the far-out version of the doctrine of Athanasius, victorious in the Western Church, which, however, modified Noetus's extremism by insisting on the distinction of three divine Persons within the divine unity. The question concerning God's and Christ's respective being issued in the famous "iota-controversy," which split the Church between those who believed in God and his Son's *sameness* of substance (*homoousia*) and those who adhered to its mere *likeness* (*homoiousia*). The most notorious modern adherent to the subordination of the Son to the Father was Newton, a semi-crypto-Arianist. (Arian was the proponent of the heresy that Athanasius opposed.) Heraclitus, speaking cutely, was a homoou-sist in the extreme; Hippolytus is right about that. The question thus has a cosmological version: Is the cosmos, in analogy to the Son, in itself divine or is it merely a divine likeness, an *image* of the Logos?

5. I might say that this conviction came to me *after* I had written the sections on, and devised the term of, "substantial relation" (Section III O–P). I got it from reading a paper by my colleague Peter Kalkavage explicating the chapter on Understanding in Hegel's *Phenomenology of Spirit*. The concept of force relevant to Heraclitus's strife, mobile or tensed, is actually that set out in Hegel's "Jena Logic" (G. W. F. Hegel, *The Jena System, 1804–5: Logic and Metaphysics*, translation edited by John W. Burbidge and George diGiovanni [Kingston and Montreal: McGill-Queen's Univ. Press, 1986], II AA, "The Relation of Substantiality," BB, note 2, pp. 54–67.) The following explicating excerpts are cited from this text: "Force unites within itself both of the essential sides of the relation, identity and separateness . . ." (p. 54). "But force is essentially the determinacy that makes substance into this determinate substance; and at the same time it is posited as connecting with what is opposed, or as having its contrary with respect to it . . . Force itself is just substance that (as relation) has

necessity in itself . . . and is inherently the unity of opposites." (p. 55). "This being of force would again be nothing but the substantiality relation itself—in other words, the necessity in which one determinacy is connected with another" (p. 59). "Force thus becomes a connection between mutually opposed, self-subsistent substances . . ." (p. 60).

Of course, within Hegelian Logic this concept of force is enmeshed in, developed from, prior terms that it would not be sensible to ascribe to Heraclitus. But taken on its own, it is very close to his meaning: that a) contesting beings, by opposing each other in strife, elicit in each other what makes them *be*—be all they can be, be vitally themselves; that b) they do so in the natural world; and that c) they are united, made one, by their mutual force relation and their reciprocal expression of power.

6. Walt Whitman, "Song of Myself," 51.

7. Adam Smith, *An Inquiry into the Nature and Causes of the Wealth of Nations* (1776), 4.2.9.

This contradictoriness of our free condition, experienced as vitalizing strife, is expressed not only as a founding principle with its germane economic theory but also in the fundamental law that actualizes them. Justice David H. Souter, in his Harvard Commencement Remarks of May 27, 2010, reflects on the question whether a certain "template for deciding constitutional claims"—that of combining evidence of facts with a "fair reading model"—could absolve the Supreme Court from the charges of "lawmaking and constitutional novelty." His answer is that there is no once-and-for-all method for settling cases because the Constitution contains provisions that are in *inherent tension* with each other, left there by the framers for future case-by-case resolutions. Its explicit terms "can create a conflict of approved values." We want the unfiltered right to publish and also the preservation of national security, freedom as well as order, liberty and also equality. "These paired desires of ours can clash," hence the Court must make choices based on current contingencies. A simplistic way of resolving conflicts "attacks our confidence, and diminishes us." In Justice Holmes's words, "repose is not our destiny."

In sum: The Constitution shows an appreciation of the Heraclitean nature of the human condition. It is held erect by self-contradiction.

Souter's "conflict of approved values" is prefigured in the "astonishing doctrine" of Plato's *Statesman* that certain genuine virtues are in ultimate opposition to each other (306b) (see *Plato's Statesman*, trans. Eva Brann, Peter Kalkavage, and Eric Salem [Newburyport, Mass.: Focus Press, 2011]).

V. The Soul of Heraclitus

1. Bywater, p. 100.
2. Galileo Galilei, *The Assayer* (1623).
3. Sigmund Freud, *The Interpretation of Dreams* (1900); Virgil, *Aeneid* 7.312.
4. There was no standing temple at Delphi from 548 B.C.E., when it burned down. It was being rebuilt during Heraclitus's lifetime (Herodotus, *Persian Wars*, 1.50, 5.62).
5. Lucian (b. 120 C.E.) makes him say: "I consider human affairs lamentable and weepable and not one of them that is not disaster-prone" (*Auction of Lives* 14, a dialogue in which the lives of philosophers go up for sale).
6. Diogenes Laertius (9.3) says that he retreated to the mountains for a while. That ultimate universalist, Kant, too, never left home, since "a city such as Königsberg on River Pregel," that has every cultural and geographic advantage, "can surely be regarded as the proper place for the expansion of human as well as world knowledge, where these can be acquired even without travel" (*Anthropology*, 1798, Preface, note).
7. Man:god::child:man,

where the ratio-relation is "being called an infant." The proportion can be written to show that it has only three terms (Euclid 5, def. 8) and is continuous:

Child:man::man:god.

In this form it displays the rise of a mature human to divinity.

Regarding the translation of *daimon*, Democritus, a contemporary of Socrates, says, to be sure:

> Happiness does not dwell in cattle or gold. Soul is the dwelling of fortune (*daimonos*). (Kirk and Raven, no. 595)

But that's, I think, in the vein of the latter-day banalization of Heraclitus, who isn't, tritely, pointing out that character trumps cattle.

For the translation of *ēthos* as a "kind," see Liddell and Scott's *Greek-English Lexicon* 2.3.

8. This fragment is terminally elusive. See Robinson (1991) for the difficulties, as well as for alternative translations and interpretations. I have stuck, as far as possible, with the way it stands.

a) "Life" and "death" seem to me cognate accusatives, as in "living a life." This construal yields the Heraclitean paradoxes "living the death" and "dying the life" that make this fragment spellbinding.

b) *Zontes*, "living," is a present participle; *tethneotes*, "having died," is a participle with past sense, for living is a process, death a state.

c) *Eikeinon*, "of those," is a demonstrative adjective pointing to the more distant of two references, be it on the page or in time and place. So it points to immortals in the first logos and to mortals in the second.

d) The clauses following the dash continue the chiastic style: ". . . living the death : the life dying . . . ," but it won't go into intelligible English.

9. The first rendering gives the sense of Diels's German translation, the second, my version, is more like Wheelwright's: "Wisdom consists in speaking and acting the truth . . ." (W 10).

Postscript

1. Kirk, p. 3.

BIBLIOGRAPHY

For an explanation of the numbering of the fragments in the text, see note 6 to Section I.

Barnes, Jonathan. *The Presocratic Philosophers: The Argument of the Philosophers*. Ed. Ted Honderich. London: Routledge, 1989.

Burnet, John. "Heraclitus of Ephesos." Chap. 3 in *Early Greek Philosophy*, pp. 130–68. Cleveland: World Publishing Company, 1961.

Bywater, I. *Heraclitus of Ephesus: Heracliti Ephesii Reliquiae*. Trans. G. T. W. Patrick. 1877, 1889. Reprint, Chicago: Argonaut Publishers, 1969.

Diels, Hermann, trans. *Die Fragmente der Vorsokratiker*. Ed. Walter Kranz. 7th ed. Vol. I. Berlin: Weidmannsche Verlagsbuchhandlung, 1954. Greek and German.

Diogenes Laertius. "Heraclitus." Bk. 9 of *Lives of Eminent Philosophers*. Trans. R. D. Hicks. Loeb Classical Library 185. Vol. 2. Cambridge: Harvard Univ. Press, 1958. Greek and English.

Gallop, David. *Parmenides of Elea: Fragments, A Text and Translation with an Introduction.* Toronto: Univ. of Toronto Press, 1984.

Guthrie, Kenneth Sylvan, comp. and trans. *The Pythagorean Sourcebook and Library: An Anthology of Ancient Writings Which Relate to Pythagoras and Pythagorean Philosophy.* Grand Rapids: Phanes Press, 1987.

Guthrie, W. K. C. "Heraclitus." Chap. 7 in *A History of Greek Philosophy*, vol. 1, pp. 403–492. Cambridge: Cambridge Univ. Press, 1962.

Hegel, G. W. F. "Die Philosophie des Heraclit." In *Vorlesungen über die Geschichte der Philosophie* (1816), vol. 1, pt. 1, sec. 1, chap. 1 D. Stuttgart: Friedrich Fromm Vorlag, 1965.

Heidegger, Martin. "Logos: Heraklit, Fragment 50" (1951). In *Vorträge und Aufsätze.* Pfullingen: Verlag Günther Neske, 1959.

———— and Eugen Fink. *Heraclitus Seminar, 1966/67.* Trans. Charles H. Seibert. University, Ala.: Univ. of Alabama Press, 1970. Also see John Sallis and Kenneth Maly, eds. *Heraclitean Fragments: A Companion Volume to the Heidegger/Fink Seminar on Heraclitus.* University, Ala.: Univ. of Alabama Press, 1980.

Heinze, Max. *Die Lehre vom Logos in der grieschischen Philosophie.* 1872. Reprint, Scientia Aalen, 1961.

Jaspers, Karl. "Heraclitus and Parmenides." In *The Great Philosophers*, pp. 15–37. Trans. Ralph Mannheim. London: Rupert Hart-Davis, 1966.

Jüngel, Bernhard. *Zum Ursprung der Analogie bei Parmenides und Heraklit.* Berlin: Walter de Gruyter, 1964.

Kahn, Charles H. "A New Look at Heraclitus." *American Philosophical Quarterly* 1, no. 3 (July 1964).

Kalkavage, Peter. "Principles of Motion and the Motion of Principles: Hegel's Inverted World." *St. John's Review* 52, no. 1 (Fall 2010), pp. 71–97.

Kirk, G. S., ed. *Heraclitus: The Cosmic Fragments.* Cambridge: Cambridge Univ. Press, 1962.

———— and J. E. Raven. *The Presocratic Philosophers: A Critical History with a Selection of Texts.* Cambridge: Cambridge Univ. Press, 1963.

Kurtz, Ewald. *Interpretationen zu den Logos-Fragmenten Heraclits.* Hildesheim: Georg Olms Verlag, 1971.

Mourelatos, Alexander P. D., ed. *The Pre-Socratics: A Collection of Critical Essays.* Sec. 4, "Heraclitus," pp. 189–238: G. S. Kirk, "Natural Change in Heraclitus"; W. K. C. Guthrie, "Flux and Logos in Heraclitus"; Hermann Fränkel, "A Thought Pattern in Heraclitus"; Uvo Hölscher, "Paradox, Simile, and Gnomic Utterance in Heraclitus." Garden City, N.Y.: Anchor Press, 1974.

Neese, Gottfried. *Heraklit Heute: Die Fragmente seiner Lehre als Urmuster europäischer Philosophie.* Hildesheim: Georg Olms Verlag, 1982.

Osborne, Catherine. "Heraclitus." Chap. 4 in *Presocratic Philosophy: A Very Short Introduction*, pp. 80–96. Oxford: Oxford Univ. Press, 2004.

Reinhardt, Karl. *Parmenides und die Geschichte der giechischen Philosophie.* 1916. Frankfurt am Main: Vittorio Klostermann, 1959. (Chap. 3, on Heraclitus's relation to Parmenides.)

————. "Heraclitea" (1942). In *Um die Begriffswelt der Vorsokratiker*, ed. Hans-George Gadamer, pp. 209–13. Darmstadt: Wissenschaftliche Buchgesellschaft, 1968.

Robb, Kevin, ed. *Language and Thought in Early Greece*: Julius M. Moravcsik, "Heraclitean Concepts and Explanations"; Kevin Robb, "Preliterate Ages and the Linguistic Art of Heraclitus." La Salle, Ill.: The Hegeler Insitute, 1983.

Robinson, T. M. *Heraclitus: Fragments, A Text and Translation with a Commentary.* Toronto: Univ. of Toronto Press, 1991.

————. "Parmenides and Heraclitus on What Can Be Known." *Revue de Philosophie Ancienne* 7, no. 2 (1989), pp. 157–67.

Rogers, Eric M. *Physics for the Inquiring Mind: The Methods, Nature, and Philosophy of Physical Science.* Princeton: Princeton Univ. Press, 1960.

Schoener, Abe. "Heraclitus and War." Lecture delivered at St. John's College, Annapolis, Md.

Seidel, George Joseph. "Heraclitus: The Logos." Chap. 5 in *Martin Heidegger and the Pre-Socratics: An Introduction to His Thought*, pp. 87–105. Lincoln: Univ. of Nebraska Press, 1964.

Slominsky, H. "Heraclit." Chap. 2 in *Heraklit und Parmenides*, pp. 7–31. Giessen: Verlag Alfred Töpelmann, 1912.

Wheelwright, Philip. *Heraclitus*. Princeton: Princeton Univ. Press, 1959.

Index of Fragments

INDEX

irrational lines, 147n. 10, 150n. 24
irrational numbers, 43

J

John the Evangelist, 111–112

K

kakotechnie (bad-skill), 29, 30
Kalkavage, Peter, 153n. 5
Kant, Immanuel, 79, 155n. 6
Keats, John: "Ode on a Grecian Urn," 52
keraunos (lightning bolt), 65, 66
"Know thyself," 26
kosmos (world-order), 30

L

Law of Contradiction, 68–69, 87, 88, 152n. 32
Law of Fixity of Composition, 55
Law of Motion, 79
legein (to collect), 10, 11
Leibniz, Gottfried, 35
listening, 15–16, 18, 21–28, 43
logic, 68–69, 149–150n. 23
logical contradictions, 27, 86–94
logical quality, 81
logos, 6, 9–13, 20; Christian use of, 13; collecting-related meanings of, 11–12; etymology of, 10; Euclidean, 36–38; prepositional prefixes of, 12; Pythagorean, 31–36; ratio-relation, 38–41; relation-related meanings of, 11, 41–44; speech-related meanings of, 10–11, 12, 92–93; translations of, 6
Logos (the), 4, 13, 15–19; vs. Being, 102–106; features of, 123; multiform, 64–70; soul and, 127–128; as speaker, 18–19, 26, 27; as West's most interesting term, 102–103
Logos fragment (50), 15–18
Lucian, 155n. 5

M

Madison, James: *Federalist Papers*, 119–121
materialism, 110
matter, 77–78
metaphor, 11, 30–31, 150n. 24; physical, 31–32; qualitative, 70–73; vs. ratio-relation, 39–40
Milesians, 9–10, 44–46, 144n. 2
money, 58–60
mortal:immortal fragment (62), 136–137, 156n. 8
motion, 47–48
multiplication, 35
musical sound, 31–34, 35, 52, 73, 148n. 17

N

necessity, 125
Newton, Isaac: *Philosophiae Naturalis Principia Math-*